A LOVE STORY

Questions and Answers on Sex

Tim Stafford

A LOVE STORY

Questions and Answers on Sex

ZONDERVAN PUBLISHING HOUSE
OF THE ZONDERVAN CORPORATION
GRAND RAPIDS, MICHIGAN 49506

CAMPUS LIFE BOOKS
A DIVISION OF YOUTH FOR CHRIST
WHEATON, ILLINOIS 60187

A LOVE STORY: QUESTIONS AND ANSWERS ON SEX
Copyright 1977 by The Zondervan Corporation
Grand Rapids, Michigan

Library of Congress Cataloging in Publication Data

Stafford, Tim.
    A love story.

    SUMMARY: Questions and answers about sex from a Christian point of view.
    1. Sex (Theology)   [1. Sex (Theology)]   I. Title.
BT708.S7   301.41   77-2136

ISBN 0-310-32971-X

Printed in the United States of America

83 84 85 86 87 88 — 15 14 13 12 11 10

Contents

Introduction

It now appears likely that within another five to ten years only a tiny minority of females and an even smaller one of males, consisting of the deeply religious, the emotionally disturbed and the personally undesirable, will remain virginal through their teens or will be virginal at the time of marriage.

Morton Hunt, *Sexual Behavior in the 1970's,*
a statistical study

The saddest love story I know is the tarantula's. In the foothills of California, near where I grew up, tarantulas come out every fall. Hideous, hairy spiders swarm everywhere. On certain roads a driver can't help squishing them under his tires. Housewives armed with brooms beat them to death. Everyone reviles them. But they still come out every fall, swarming by the millions.

If that sounds more like a horror story than a love story, it's because you don't know much about tarantulas. They don't live up to their fierce image. Actually, they would rather hide under a bush than jump out and bite you. And their bite is not particularly poisonous. They are solitary, oversized, ungainly creatures, so heavy they can break a leg in a fall. They are friendly (or as friendly as a spider less heroic than Charlotte can be), make good pets, and will even take to being walked on a leash. And they are virtually blind.

So how does a poor, blind spider, living a solitary life under a pile of brush, find a mate? The answer, apparently, is that some autumn instinct sends him wandering haplessly across the countryside, bumping into everything in his path, risking terrified housewives and speeding cars until he bumps into a tarantula of the opposite sex. Without much vision, and without extraordinary powers of hearing or scent, he has to establish contact by touch.

So it is really only by accident that two tarantulas find each other. The fact that there are so many tarantulas, and that they try so desperately, keeps the tarantula race intact. But most tarantulas never find a suitable love at all; they go bumping across the landscape until the end of their forlorn days.

They are not so different from us. Perhaps the tarantula, rather than the cherub, should be the symbol of romantic love for us human beings. Most of us look desperately for love. We don't know how to look; our senses don't lead us very well, so we wander across our landscape hoping to bump into it. We take many risks, and the "losers" are strewn everywhere. But there is no time for pity. We keep rushing along, bumping into people and checking them out (often, like the spider, by touch), hoping to find the right mate. Some of us succeed. But a large proportion of us never find that true love we dream of.

We make sad, or at best dull, love stories with our lives.

A few years ago I started writing about sex. I was talked into it by my fellow editors at *Campus Life* magazine. I didn't pretend to know a lot about it. I knew one thing: sex is very important. It is one of the greatest sources of pleasure and pain we know. More than that, our society's view of it is up for grabs. People used to assume that the Christian way was simply the right way. They might have violated the rules, but they still respected them. Those days are gone. Now, many people doubt whether Christian rules have any value at all.

At *Campus Life* we try to deal realistically with problems, so I kept saying, "We've got to deal with sex. Even if we don't solve all the problems, we've got to at least talk about them. If we ignore sex, we've put 'spirituality' in a little compartment where it will shrivel up and die."

My fellow editors believed me, and that's why I am writing about sex.

It scares me. Sex is a big, difficult subject. Writing about it makes me feel more than a little foolish. I am not an expert. I have never taken a course on sex. I am not married. I am not a counselor with thousands of case experiences to draw from. I have not lived long enough to have the benefit of wisdom or long-distance perspective. I have neither the advantage of having lived the ideal life of Christian sexuality nor the advantage of having sinned so often that I know all the ways one can go wrong. My life, sexually at least, is similar to that of millions of others: I've stumbled along, doing my best.

You might wonder, then, why I am trying to write a book on a subject I know so little about. I sometimes wonder that myself. But let me point out a couple of small advantages I have.

First, I can read, and I can talk. When I first got the assignment to write a column about sex for *Campus Life* magazine I was scared enough to go out and read anything I could get my hands on. I've read a lot more since — all kinds of books, magazines, articles, etc. I've read *Playboy* philosophy. I've read statistical analyses of the sexual revolution. I've read middle-of-the-road articles in magazines like *Seventeen* warning you to make sure you're "responsible" about sex. And I've read a great deal of what other Christians have written, from the heavily theological to the "all-right-guys-and-gals" school of practical advice for teens. I've also talked to many people, from "experts" to kids who've been to bed enough times to think they're experts. From all that, I've learned a lot.

Not much in this book is original. Nearly everything is from someone else — often from two or three other people. I've tried to bring together many Christian insights from a number of people, and make them interesting, clear, and relevant to what people want to know. I've tried to get it to make sense.

My other advantage is that, since I'm young, I haven't forgotten what questions people really ask. I remember the sex education book my parents gave me. It did tell the facts of life. Barely. To find them, you had to do a lot of dull reading about dating and courtship, about responsibility and maturity and God. Only because I desperately wanted to know about the birds and the bees did I have the patience to comb through that entire book. I finally found, in the back, those three or four cryptic sentences that described in totally clinical terms the sexual act.

Books about sex morality can be like that, too. It isn't that what they're saying is unimportant. It's just that they answer questions no one is asking. This book tries to deal fully with questions people ask. First on the list is, "What's wrong with sex now?"

I believe if you really want to get the most satisfaction out of being a sexual person (which you are — God made you that way), Christianity offers the best way of going about it. That is not a common viewpoint today. Statistically, those handling sex the Christian way are a minority. In the average classroom you'll get snickered at for suggesting premarital sex is wrong. Those old beliefs seem to be the exclusive property of preachers, priests, parents, and old maids.

Because of that, this book will not defend the Christian point of view. Defending implies a certain mental attitude: defensiveness. Some wonderful people are still defending the Christian way, but they don't understand that the battle has already passed them. They're defending a small, sagging fort in enemy territory, and they don't have the manpower to influence things outside their walls. They're barely holding the fort.

We can learn from the attitude Mao Tse-tung took. He knew his ideas weren't majority ideas. He knew better than to try to establish and defend a fort. Instead, he said that the common people were the sea, and his men the fish that swam in it. His men didn't make themselves conspicuous. But they were around. They were always planting ideas in the heads of those who would listen. They did it courteously. Initially they didn't force their ideas on others. They couldn't. They were in a minority. But they were very sure what they believed was right.

So instead of defending Christian ideas, I am going to propose them. Right now a half-dozen ideas about how to handle our sexuality are with us. Each one seems to work for at least some people. If it didn't, no one would follow it for very long. Each system of ideas has some advantages, and each, Christianity included, has some disadvantages. There is no way of handling sex that doesn't involve pain somewhere or sometime — that's just not the way life is. You always have to give up something to get something better.

I believe that when you add up all the columns, Jesus' ideas on sex come out ahead of anyone else's. You do give up some things. You have to cope with the frustration of waiting, for instance. But there are worse kinds of frustration.

My column for *Campus Life* magazine is called "Love, Sex and the Whole Person." I've gotten hundreds and hundreds of letters from people in pain. They're people looking for love, unhappy with what they're finding. Some of their letters are funny, their problems absurd. Others seem just sad. Some letters come in misspelled scrawls and a child's grammar; many come on pink or flowered stationery; some come neatly typed on clean white bond. Each letter represents a human being, usually a person without anyone to whom he or she can talk honestly.

You are going to meet a number of these people through their letters. All the letters in this book are real, and most of their questions are common ones. I think you will find that some represent you.

Let me say something about the religious basis of this

book. If you're not committed to Jesus Christ, some of it may turn you off. I hope it won't. I don't think you absolutely have to believe in Jesus to agree with what the Bible says about sex.

It's sad that Christianity and the Bible have gotten the reputation of being completely opposed to pleasurable sex. Most people don't think of God as the type who would enjoy it.

But the one basic fact we believe about God and sex is that He invented it. It was His idea, complete with all its excitement and passion.

That should change some of our ideas about God. There is a world of difference between using something often and inventing it. I have achieved almost 100% efficiency in using the electric light. I can turn it on with the air of the sophisticated expert — and baby, it really shines. But I have only the foggiest idea of how it works. I'd have to get a book to figure out how to wire it. And I *know* I wouldn't have had the ingenuity to invent it. If it were left to me, we'd still be using candles.

Some of us get to thinking we are pretty liberated about sex. We learn how to use it effectively, or at least think we do. But not one of us has a sufficiently wild imagination to have thought it up.

After all, God could have let us reproduce as plants do. I could take my fingernail clippings, stick them in the ground, and in nine months (assuming the weather was good) out would come babies. It might be fun for a time or two. It might be a friendly way to reproduce, with all the ease and relaxation of growing tomatoes. But it would be rather dull. It wouldn't show much passion. It wouldn't bring two people intimately into each other's arms. It wouldn't be the sort of thing you'd lie awake thinking about.

God thought our kind of sex would be more worthwhile. That's why He made us as He did.

That brings us again to the point of this book. It's not to tell you what you shouldn't do.

It's not to keep you from fun.

It's to open you to the freedom of passionate, loving sex in the best way possible.

1
Why Wait?

Why . . . should *this* kind of juncture of two bodies be so much more serious than *this* kind — say, shaking hands?

Thomas Howard, *An Antique Drum*

Nobody can really do what the prostitute and her customer try; nobody can go to bed with someone and leave his soul parked outside.

Lewis Smedes, *Sex for Christians*

My girl friend and I are juniors in college. We have gone together since we were freshmen, and have restrained ourselves as far as having sex is concerned. Last spring we got engaged. We plan to be married as soon as we graduate.

But it has been harder and harder to keep from going all the way. Sometimes Julie and I talk about it and we feel really frustrated. Lately she's been saying things like "I wish I could understand what's wrong with it." It's not like she comes out and says she'd like to have sex, but I think if I wanted to she'd be willing. And really, I want to, but I'm also afraid. I've always expected to wait for marriage. Now I'd feel better if we just went ahead. Then at least we wouldn't be frustrated.

I'M STARTING WITH this question because it includes all the "What-if?" factors. I spent four years in coed dorms, and I've sat in hours-long discussions trying to hold up the Christian outlook on sex. I know how the arguments go. I've had mine battered with that insistent "What-if?"

"*What if* they're using birth control, and there's no fear of pregnancy? Then would it be right?"

"*What if* they really love each other, and don't feel any guilt?"

"*What if* they're going to get married?"

"What's wrong with sex before marriage, if sex is supposed to be beautiful?"

Good questions, all of them. So consider this guy who wrote to me. You have to feel compassion for him. He and his fiancée are planning to be married. Presumably they really love each other, and aren't just infatuated. Presumably they are thoughtful enough to use birth control effectively, and don't have to worry about VD. Besides which, it appears to them that waiting for marriage is tearing up their relationship. The frustration is too much to take.

I could have started with a more typical case: a pair of high school juniors who've been together three months, feel madly in love, and think they might go all the way soon. The typical couple is a lot younger, less thoughtful and less committed than the couple who wrote to me. Often one is more crazy about sex than about his partner, or they are both more in love with love than with each other. If so, you can expect their relationship to split within a few months.

But I want to take on the ideal situation. If premarital sex is a bad idea for this engaged couple, it's bad for everyone.

I'm going to assume all the "What-ifs?" by considering this couple first. And I'm also going to assume one thing about you: you're not interested in a second-rate relationship. I assume you're searching for the most loving, sexually fulfilling relationship two humans are capable of — marriage as marriage is meant to be, and not as it is commonly lived.

I say "marriage" because I can't see any way around it. If you are in love with someone that deeply, you're going to want to live together. You're going to want to share everything. And you're certainly not going to be content to let the relationship drop after a few years. You're going to want to stay together forever, if it's that good. If your goal is the best, you'll ultimately choose the state of committed living together we call marriage.

Unless that is your goal, what I say won't help much. I can't prove to you that sex before marriage will make you miserable. I can't prove you will end up tearing out your hair from the guilt. You know better. Some people do end up miserable, but you know others who have sex and don't regret it.

But I believe they are missing something. They are missing their best chance at the deep, soul-satisfying love we all want. Even this couple, in love and engaged to be married, is in danger of missing out on the best. I'm going to list six reasons why couples ought to wait.

1). When you're in love, the frustration of waiting is hard to take. But have you thought of the ways it could help your relationship?

For one thing, sex is a way of expressing love. But it's not the only way, or even the most helpful. To build a relationship takes time — time talking and doing things together. When you're sleeping together but not living together, sex tends to take over to the exclusion of other ways of expressing love. But when you put off sex, you can channel that love energy into getting to know each other better.

The best relationships aren't formed in pressure-free

environments anyway. Yes, waiting for sex can be frustrating, but many things in life are frustrating. The question is, what as a couple do you do with those pressures? Do you handle them creatively? Do they tear you apart or push you closer together? If you can't learn to help each other grow through this pressure, are you really suited to help each other through the other pressures of life? Marriage ultimately is going to force you to "wait" on many things you want.

Waiting doesn't have to be grim. If you see it as a challenge, it can almost be fun. And it certainly is good experience.

2). An engagement period is, by its nature, a period of testing — of partial commitment. You still can back out, and whether you like to believe it or not, you might. Something like 50% of the people who get married have been engaged at least once before. That means many engagements don't work out. If you do break up, it will be much more painful if you've already had sex together. Breaking any engagement is traumatic; with sex involved, it can be worse. Do you want to risk that pain? Or risk it for your fiancée?

This is true for any relationship, engaged or not: breaking up when you've had sex together is much more emotionally tearing. Sex brings you together in ways you can't predict. It does change you. We all know, somewhere inside, that those who have made love weren't meant to be torn apart. But there is no guarantee anywhere — not in feelings of love, not in the words "I love you," not even in an engagement — that your relationship is going to go all the way to marriage.

3). Intercourse is not necessarily that wonderful the first few times, even in marriage. It takes time (often years), patience, and ideal conditions for many people to have a genuinely fulfilling experience.

The Sorenson Report, the most complete sociological study of teenage sexuality available, asked girls who had had their first intercourse before marriage to choose words to describe their reaction. They chose words like "afraid," "guilty," "worried," and "embarrassed" before any others. Words like "happy," "joyful," and "satisfied" came substantially further down the list. No one is saying your fiancée will feel like that, but the odds are for it. Have you considered the complications it will bring to your relationship if your first sex experience is bad for one or both of you?

It's hard enough to handle failure like that inside marriage. Outside, there is little time to deal with it. Unless you're living together, you've got to get dressed and separate. And you lack the security about the future that newlyweds feel, having just said their vows. You also usually lack the privacy and security that are likely to help sexual success along. Failures are more likely outside marriage than in. And they're complicated by the problem of guilt, which sneaks in and surprises people when they least expect it. The result of having sexual failures now could be a lot harder on both of you than the present frustrations. It could even break up your relationship.

4). If you're planning marriage, you must be looking forward to a whole new life of sharing together. It's not just sex, of course: it's *life*. That includes work, cooking, choosing where to live, vacations, and probably even the creation of new human beings. It's a whole: sex can't be separated from the rest of it, and you don't want to separate it.

When you're thinking in terms of a lifetime, the year or so of your engagement is a relatively short period. How do you want that lifetime to begin? With a great celebrative party, or furtively, secretly? Do you want to sneak into sex, or would you rather start with a honeymoon to enjoy it, with all the time and privacy in the world? Do you want it to begin when you're only partly sure you're doing the right thing, when there are still some doubts in the back of your mind? Or when you stand together in front of all your friends and say, in effect, "It's right for us to be together for all time, and we're completely dedicated to that. You help us and hold us to it." The contrast between the two ways of beginning is so great, it seems to me to be worth quite a bit of waiting.

5). By having sex you're relieving the frustration of putting it off, but you're also relaxing the attractive tension that keeps you together.

The sexes are called opposite because in many ways they are. Usually they have different ways of looking at things.

They have different interests. Yet there is an attraction that brings them together.

Think of the most boring subject you can. Algebra? Copper production? Then put yourself in a small room with an attractive member of the opposite sex to talk about that subject. I'll guarantee that subject will acquire a sudden fascination.

Sure, it's biological. Most people don't feel it until they're older than twelve. But it's nothing to be ashamed of. It's something to be excited about and thankful for, because God made it to be that way. I'm not really talking about the need for release from sexual tension. Sexual attraction goes far beyond that. It's the desire to probe and understand the mystery of another person. It's the kind of tingling conversation in which you want to talk and listen at the same time, in which you want to swallow sentences whole. It's an intense, unsatisfiable curiosity, a sense that you're being drawn up and out of yourself into a whole new world you have to explore; it's an itch that is pure joy to scratch but that can't ever be scratched enough. And sexual intercourse is the culmination of this urge. It's a delightful, healthy urge, and a practical one too: it brings male and female together. And it keeps them together, urging them to put more time and effort into exploring the other's personality.

But what happens if you go all the way with the urge? What happens if you have sex?

Several things can happen. First, powerful emotions can appear. They're different for different people. Some feel naked and ashamed. Others feel confused and bewildered. Often people suddenly feel as though their partner is a stranger to them. There is the distinct feeling, for many, that something has changed; they have "lost" something. Intercourse turns out to be more than something physical. They thought it would be simply one step beyond making out, but it turns out to be a spiritual act. What it comes down to, I think, is a feeling of having stumbled into a place you never imagined existed, and for which you weren't ready.

It's a strange experience, even in marriage, when your partner and you "know" each other as well as you possibly can, and have committed yourselves unbreakably to each other. Outside of marriage, it sometimes makes you feel as though you've made yourself naked for a stranger.

And that can be followed in time by boredom. You have gone "all the way." There's no more mystery about your partner: you've satisfied your curiosity. Or so you think. Actually, sex in that sense is lying to you. It doesn't reveal anything: it only expresses what love and understanding is already there. Nevertheless, you feel as though the relationship is fulfilled, and sooner or later you begin to realize it isn't all that fulfilling. You've done the ultimate, and the ultimate wasn't enough. No curiosity or desire to probe the mystery of the other person pulls you back together. Boredom sets in.

This doesn't happen right away. Sex is meant, after all, to be the ultimate expression of love, and it certainly can feel like it. The first time it may be tremendous. Even if it isn't tremendous, at least it's the first time. That in itself is exciting.

But that can change with time. Your relationship tends to plateau at the level it has already reached. You don't lose interest in sex, but if your relationship isn't very deep, you do lose interest in your partner. Your curiosity is gone. Much of your time together is dominated by sex. No longer is intense energy put into exploring each other's personality. Eventually a breakup comes, often painfully. Or (what may be worse) you go on to marriage simply from a sense of duty. The joy is gone.

Of course, some of this attractive tension dies with married couples too. But there are a million other things to hold you together then — legal things, social things, the fact that you live together and share everything. And the fact that you share all of life forces you to continue to explore each other, to grow. That growth revives the attraction, giving it new dimensions.

So the issue is this: are you willing to put up with the frustration of waiting in order to make sure that your relationship becomes everything it was meant to? Most people in our society answer no. They say no to any sacrifice, starting with refusing to wait for sex and ending with a refusal to stick to and work for a good marriage when things get difficult. The results are obvious: millions of lonely lives.

One other thing:

6). Premarital sex will erode your relationship with God.

Maybe you don't care. If not, skip this. But if God means much to you, then this fact may affect you more than anything else.

You can't listen to what God says and go out and do the opposite too often. The joy of relating to Him will fade. Prayer and Christian fellowship will mean less. They usually will die a quiet death. You may not even realize it until you wake up in the middle of the night and wonder where God has gone.

Before going out with me, my boyfriend dated lots of girls. I had a few boyfriends too, but never any serious relationships.

Since our relationship started, we have made love numerous times, though we waited until we had grown to love each other very much. Since we have made love, our relationship has grown. We have really serious talks about life – religion, economics, politics, music, art, sports, etc. But we primarily talk about our future together.

We are freshmen in different colleges, planning to do our undergraduate work in less than four years and then work a year before we marry.

We didn't want our relationship based on physical attraction, so we stopped making love four months ago while we further developed other aspects of our God-centered relationship. We have grown tremendously: we're trusting, understanding, and very patient with each other. And we have both grown spiritually.

But we both feel that engaging in sex is for people who are in love as we are. We have asked the Lord about it and read the Bible to find concrete answers, but we've been very unsuccessful. Every time we are together we want to express our love for each other. If it's wrong, we will restrain. But it is so hard, because we've been there before and we know how fulfilling sex is to our relationship. We feel as though we're already married because 1) we're in love and 2) we've accomplished something by communicating which some married people don't accomplish until *they've been married for quite some time.*

And what is marriage anyway? Why do we have to have a piece of paper to have sex? Marriage is supposed to be based on love. We have love – are we wrong in having sex?

THIS LETTER IS the kind that seldom finds its way into books telling why people should wait for sex until marriage. Of course, assuming what you say is all true, you are a rarity. Not many find that premarital sex deepens their relationship and brings them closer to God. Not many go beyond where married couples have gone in their love. I could quibble, and doubt whether what you are saying is true, but I don't know you, and have to take your word for it. Actually, I don't doubt that as far as you or anyone else could see, what you are saying is true.

But I still think you would be wiser to wait.

The main reason is that I don't believe God meant sex to celebrate a state of half-marriage. Sex was meant to express and celebrate the real thing — and sex is most satisfying in the fully-married context. You probably wouldn't disagree; it's just that you essentially feel you're married, and lack only a piece of paper.

I can understand the disgust some people feel when they're told to let a piece of paper define the way they express their love. They are the same people the day before and the day after the wedding. What does legalese and ink and paper have to do with *love,* for heaven's sake? Love is warm and human; ink and paper are cold and inanimate.

Let's forget about that for a moment and talk about the way the Bible sees marriage. There were no legal documents in Bible times. Even if you don't believe the Bible is God's Word, consider it a potential source of wisdom.

The Bible says relatively little about marriage or sex but it does have one key sentence repeated three times. The sentence describes the first marriage, and it is quoted by both Jesus and Paul when they talk about marriage. It goes like this: "Therefore a man shall leave his father and his mother, and shall cleave unto his wife; and they shall be one flesh." Jesus adds to that, "What therefore God hath joined together, let not man put asunder."

The verse from Genesis 2 contains three parts. First, "the man shall leave his father and his mother." It was assumed in Old Testament times that the wife would leave her family at marriage. This verse makes a point of saying the man would also. In other words, marriage is a new beginning. In every culture, however marriage is defined, this is true. There may not be a ceremony, but nevertheless a new unit is formed in society, and people know it.

Walter Trobisch has written that in some African tribes, the entire village dances along with the groom when he leaves his village to go to another for his bride. There are no legal documents (nor were there any in the Old Testament). There is no license, no piece of paper. But everyone knows what has happened, and stands behind the marriage. The people reinforce responsibility to the partner, to any potential children, and to society in general. That's what's implied by "the man shall leave his mother and his father."

Then comes the phrase "cleave unto his wife." What does "cleave" mean? It means to stick together, like two pieces of paper glued so that they can't be separated without tearing. It means a complete sharing — of money, time, thoughts, and emotions. It means total commitment.

Then, only after naming these things, do we have the phrase "be one flesh." Some people read this as a nice way of saying "have sex." But the Bible is not very spinsterish about sex: if it wanted to put it more plainly I think it would. "One flesh," or "one body" implies sex, but more than sex. It implies a union of persons that goes beyond the purely physical action. In a sense it is saying two people become one person through the activity of sex.

That's marriage. How it is formalized depends on the culture. In ours it is done, usually, with a wedding ceremony in which certain promises are made in front of witnesses. It usually includes a celebration for good friends and family. And it is a legal action which you can be dragged into court for violating. In a society where people live in small towns and don't move much, that paper legality may not be necessary. The village or tribe naturally enforces a marriage agreement (so that, for instance, the wife doesn't get stuck supporting children whenever her husband gets the urge to take off). In our society, sadly, we have to rely on the anonymity of the courts.

But let's not be romantic and pretend we can do without that legal protection. There are simply too many ways people can be hurt. And more than that, the law reinforces the promises made to love and cherish. There are always days in any marriage when love isn't very strong. The "piece of paper" helps keep things together until another day when things look better. The piece of paper isn't to keep lovers from loving each other. It's to make sure that lovers who are really serious keep on loving each other. It holds love in.

Now, I've known people who approximated marriage by making promises to each other — private promises. Maybe they even gave a ring. That sounds attractive. It's a verbal commitment without the apparent coldness of a piece of paper.

But think about it. One thing I hate to bring up is that some people are liars. Guys in particular seem capable of saying things they know aren't true for the sake of sex. The Sorenson Report stated that more than a third of the sexually experienced girls believed when they first had sex they would marry the guy (though few of them did). But only 7% of the guys said the same thing. Either someone wasn't telling the truth, or someone else was fooling herself.

And even if both of you have perfectly pure motives, you have to admit that we all make vows we don't keep. I may vow to lose ten pounds roughly every other week. In the emotion of the moment, I really mean it. But I don't keep the promise.

One way to strengthen any promise I make is to do it publicly. The more of my friends and family I make the promise to, the more you can bet I'll keep the promise. And if you remind me that I'm promising this not just to people, but also to God Himself, you have an even stronger promise. Why? Because I feel responsible to God and those people, and I know they'll hold me to my promise.

And there's another way to strengthen a promise. Get it on paper. Get it notarized. Have some money standing behind it that you'll forfeit if you don't follow through.

Sometimes I loan money to friends. If it's a little money, like for lunch, I don't really care whether I get it back. I trust the person. Usually I get it back, though often enough, even with good friends, I don't. But it's not a big deal.

Suppose I were loaning something significant: a large sum of money I really needed. I might be loaning to the best friend in the world, but if I wanted to make absolutely sure he would keep this promise to return the money, I think I would have him sign a legal note. That would hold him better to his promise, and I could afford to take the risk of the loan.

I think wedding promises have something in common with that. Making them legal doesn't have to make them cold, but it does reinforce them.

I realize it does seem cold to even talk about risks in the future. Why not just love spontaneously? If we really love, why not trust each other totally for the future? Or if we really want to split later, is the relationship worth saving anyway?

That may be the way it was in the Garden of Eden. If people were completely good, we would have no use for laws (though we might, just for the pleasure, celebrate weddings with parties and promises. Lovers tend to promise things to each other anyway, without any legal prodding).

But we know that we are fickle and selfish lovers. We wish we could be stronger, loving constantly and unselfishly without outside help. But it doesn't work that way. We need all the prodding we can get. Even with the help of the wedding ceremony, and even with the help of God, many people can't love enough to make a strong marriage.

We also know that the way we feel one moment shouldn't be allowed to run our whole lives. This is why the idea "when affection's gone, there's no point to going on" is so false. We're fickle. One moment we love, and the next we don't. Every married person knows what it is to get up in the morning and find his or her partner as attractive as a slug. But the only way we find the deepest fulfillment of our need for love is to keep trying, again and again, letting every failure spur us on to grow closer.

So where can we place you in this discussion? One thing ought to be clear: you are not married. You fulfill one part: you are "one flesh" in that you have had sex. But you have only partly learned what it is to cleave — to be joined together and love each other in every practical area of life. Cleaving is down-to-earth work. One obvious aspect is living together, sharing the chores and the money. (Don't underestimate that one — money means much to us Americans. If we haven't learned to share it totally, and also share the problems that come when it runs out, we aren't cleaving.)

You have barely begun to "leave your parents" and make a new, public, social unit. You are barely halfway to marriage, as the Bible sees it. Marriage is much more than just being "in love," as wonderful as love is, and as far in it as you've come. Where will the joy of your wedding day be? You will most likely be taking on the drearier responsibilities of love while the new joy and communication that's supposed to be a part and parcel — sexual intercourse — will be something old.

What's more, you may never make it that far. Without some of the dreary responsibilities, without the total sharing and practical life together, the joys of sex won't have much content to nourish you. Sex may get old, and so may your relationship. The boredom other unmarried lovers experience may come just as easily for you, no matter how your love has grown. Love can never stay in one place. Either it goes forward or it falls back. And when it falls back, what will you have to strengthen it with? How far can your love grow when you're separated, when your love-making is furtive and part time, when the most challenging choice your love faces is which movie to attend?

There is an option. You could get married. Why don't you?

I would use your answers as the reasons you are not really ready for marriage.

You might answer with things like, "We're too young," "We don't have the money yet," or "We need to finish school." But those are obstacles which can be overcome if you are willing to sacrifice: one can put the other through school. Perhaps you really don't feel ready for marriage. You are not ready for that total a responsibility, that final a commitment.

Realistically, I wouldn't give a couple just starting college a ten percent chance of waiting for each other on separate campuses for five years. I've seen too many of those romances break up. And sex won't strengthen the bond. As I've explained, it's more likely to weaken it.

One other thing. Your letter points out, realistically, how much harder it is to avoid sex once you've experienced it. People sometimes suggest that occasionally releasing sexual steam will make us less sexually compulsive. I doubt that. From what I can see, sex builds on sex. The more we practice it, the more we need to practice it.

So even conceding that sex was a mistake in the first place, you might say it's too hard to stop. In other words, once you've taken the wrong road, you might as well keep on driving as turn around and go back to the point where you took the wrong turn.

It is hard to stop, especially once you've begun. But if it can be done, it's better for you. And I have good news for you: it can be done. Not alone. Not one of you wanting to and the other not. Not even a team of the two of you working against all your sexual impulses. But with the two of you plus God and Christian friends, you can do anything.

If *a couple has sex and then later goes ahead and gets married, is it a sin?*

YES, IT IS — nothing you do later can make up for a sin. A thief who gives the money back is not allowed to walk away free. He's still a thief. It takes God's efforts — not our own — to make us over again.

But I suppose you are wondering what difference the date of the wedding ceremony makes. After all, if a couple went through with the promises, they must have been serious about them all along. And doesn't that make all the difference?

Well, it certainly makes some difference. Having sex with your fiancée is not as serious a mistake as having sex casually with someone you felt momentarily in love with. But it is still a mistake.

Let's take the ultimate case. Suppose I were getting married June 29, and I and my fiancée got carried away the night before, June 28. Would I be in the wrong just because I was a few hours ahead of the scheduled ceremony?

I doubt this kind of premarital sex poses a serious threat to marriage, and therefore I doubt if God is most concerned about it. But there is a principle involved — cheating a nickel on your income tax is still cheating — and we need forgiveness for all kinds of thoughts and petty sins that may not seem terribly destructive. For violating promises we made to God or each other, my fiancee and I would need to be forgiven.

But the principle isn't what I'd worry most about. I would worry about the motives involved. Why a day early? Why not wait for the perfect moment? What happened to self-control? Wouldn't the motive be simply sexual desire, uncontrolled by love?

Why not wait? You can, and it will be well worth the trouble just for the beauty of the right moment.

Some people say how having sex broke up what they thought was a great relationship. They thought their love was real, but after they had sex things deteriorated.

But how do you know the same thing wouldn't happen after marriage if they'd waited? Couldn't you use sex as a means to establish whether that relationship will hold true after marriage and forever?

IT'S A HARD test you're suggesting, because breaking up after having sex is especially painful and confusing. However, if sex were really a good test, and there were no alternatives, it might be worth taking the chance, since finding the right person to spend your life with is as important as anything you'll ever do.

But is sex an effective test? Not really. Why did those who had sex before marriage break up? Not necessarily because sex showed them they weren't going with the right person. In many cases the power of sex overwhelmed their relationship, and also removed the one thing that would have kept them coming back together: the mystery of the other person. If they hadn't gone all the way, it's possible some of them could have built their relationship to the point where they really did want to go "all the way" to marriage. Some of them probably spoiled a relationship that would have had greater potential if they hadn't been in such a hurry.

Sex poses as a great test of compatibility because it's a very important part of marriage. People usually figure if they're not sexually compatible, they can't have a good marriage. And why not find out before it's too late?

There are two problems with that. One is, you can't tell. Just because sex isn't satisfying before marriage doesn't say much about what it will be later, with all the advantages of security, time, privacy, and certainty about the future. Most couples say it takes years to work out their sexual adaptation.

Also good sex is no ironclad guarantee of later sexual happiness. People have been known to fake sexual enjoyment to please their partner. For another thing, changes come: the fact that sex is exciting and pleasurable now is no guarantee it'll still be exciting and pleasurable five hundred experiences later. To *stay* exciting sex requires an exciting, growing relationship. Nothing you do in bed before marriage tests that. The time you spend together out of bed is a far better test.

The trouble is, we have the idea that sexual compatibility is something built into our genes. Sex therapists have pretty thoroughly discarded that theory. Compatibility doesn't relate to sexual organs — there are almost no couples whose organs aren't adequately suited physically to each other. The problems most couples have with sex relate strongly to other parts of their relationship — their ability to communicate, their willingness to be unselfish in love, and their understanding and love for their partner. Sexual technique is significant, too, but it's different with each person. These are elements you can't test. You can only work them out. And naturally they're best worked out in the finest environment possible: marriage.

That does leave marriage as something of a risk. And that

shouldn't surprise you. Life is a risk too. Look at it this way: the wedding ceremony isn't the end of the adventure. It's the beginning. Up until the ceremony, all you've done is selected your traveling companion and the equipment you'll need. There is no possible guarantee you'll deal well with the problems that arise. The only helpful preparation is to know each other deeply, know how to communicate when you're under stress, and become the best possible human beings you can. Don't try to remove the risks of marriage (or any other relationship). Get in shape so that you can face problems when they come.

I*'ve always felt sex is a gift from the Lord, not to be used or abused. I realize many times lust and dirt take over our minds. Making love is meant to be very beautiful in the minds of those involved. Maybe this is why so many say to wait until after marriage.*

Yet I feel you can make love to someone before marriage, as long as love is there and lust has not entered. When love is put across this way, how can it be said to be dirty? Or do I have the wrong idea of true love, faithfulness, and beauty?

YOU CERTAINLY ARE on the right track. Sex and love are meant to go together.

But I don't think you go far enough. I get all kinds of letters from people who are "in love." Some of them sound so incredibly naive you would probably laugh if you read them. Others sound mature and committed. People mean different things by love.

It's not so easy to tell "puppy love" from the real thing, especially when you're the one in love. In fact, I doubt if anyone ever feels more desperately lost in love than a 13-year-old guy mooning over the girl who sits behind him in English. So if you judge these things by how much in love you feel, is that 13-year-old ready for sex?

Most people think of love as something that comes and goes. It zaps you with good feelings, and suddenly you're in love and the world is wonderful. Of course, it also disappears, and then there's nothing you can do to reclaim it. Perhaps it'll come back . . . perhaps you'll be one of those "lucky" people who finds a lifelong love. But that seems mostly left up to chance. (Remember the tarantulas?)

If that kind of love really made sex okay, it would be difficult to tell whether you had enough of it. We can't wire you up to test how powerful those love feelings are. All we can do is take you at your word — and you don't really know either, because you can't compare your feelings with anyone else's feelings. You can never be totally sure of your partner's feelings, nor can you ever know how long either of yours will last.

So you do what most people do — you wing it. Depending on how strong your morals are, and depending on how strong the feelings get, you end up making love and hoping for the best. If the relationship doesn't work out — well, that's the chance you take. Your commitment to each other was based on the "in love" feelings. When they go away, so does your commitment.

Those romantic, come-and-go love feelings are lovely things, and innocent in themselves. Few things feel better than being in someone's arms thinking you've finally found real love. But the feelings are unreliable. They make a shaky foundation for a relationship. They're more like the whipped cream on top of the sundae than the glass that holds things together. A relationship that lasts takes time and work, and come-and-go love is the antithesis of those things — it comes and goes when and how it likes, regardless of what you do.

If you think this kind of love is all sex needs, I'd have to disagree. It's good, but it's not enough.

So what kind of love *does* make sex okay? I think it's the love of total commitment. I call it forever love. It's the kind of love that lasts forever, because it's love that refuses to be stopped by hurt feelings, by failures, or by attractions you feel for a third person. Forever love doesn't just happen to you. It's something you decide on, and commit yourself to.

Of course, there's a trick to knowing whether you have this love, too. Your feelings can fool you. You can feel pretty committed one day and then discover the next day you aren't.

So how do you really know? Magazines like *The Reader's Digest* occasionally print 20-question "tests" that allow you to check on how mature your commitment is. They're not bad, but there is one test that is much more reliable: marriage. If you are ready to marry, making a vow before your friends and God, agreeing to share everything forever, then there is a better chance your love is really committed.

Obviously, by "marriage" I mean more than a piece of paper. I'm talking about the commitment to stay with each other lovingly, no matter what.

Why are people so against making this permanent commitment? Why do they talk as though it's such a rigid and moralistic requirement? It's really a natural outgrowth of love; left to ourselves, we would have to invent marriage all over again. Why? Because sexual pleasures increase to the degree that they last. A brief encounter with a beautiful girl doesn't touch the potential of spending my whole life with her, growing in love. The longer we're together, and the better we know each other, the deeper the pleasure gets. A week together is better than a day; a year than a week; a lifetime than a year.

Of course, it works the other way too. The pain of ending a casual acquaintance of the opposite sex is nothing compared to the pain I get when rejected by someone I care about. And a wrecked marriage is much more painful than that. So one ought to be very careful.

Perhaps you feel I haven't answered the question, "What's *dirty* about sex where there's love?" There isn't necessarily anything dirty. But what kind of love is it? And how do you know? The surest test is total, public commitment.

I agree that the best sex is for marriage. I know sexual relationships outside of marriage don't mean that much to me, if I'm honest. I say they'll last forever, but I know they won't.

But I think when the right person comes, I'll know it. Then I'll act differently. What's wrong with that?

THIS IS THE myth current today: that it's all right to have some casual affairs (as long as there's some love involved) while looking for the magic prince or princess to come along. Then forever love will be natural. You'll get married and live happily ever after.

Sometimes it does work that way, but usually it doesn't. Two strong factors work against it.

First is the fact that there is no "love at first sight." That is, there is no "forever love" at first sight. You can fall in love immediately — but forever love is a building thing, growing as you become familiar with each other's thoughts, habits, and rhythms. Each time a problem comes up and you're able to solve it together, your love grows.

So there is no way to know, at the beginning, whether you've found the right person. Your magic princess will look just like all the others. Only patient, careful love will help you discover whether you're right for each other. Your casual partner might have been meant to be your permanent partner. But through casualness you can miss her, or hurt her badly.

The other factor is habit. Most of us fall in love a number of times. Each time we hope we've found the right one. But only time tells, and usually time tells us to look for someone else.

However, you don't shrug those relationships off. You carry away habits, which are very powerful. They can be very good. A person who learns to treat all members of the opposite sex lovingly and respectfully develops character. But the habits can also be very destructive.

Can you really believe that people who've had a variety of come-and-go lovers, sex and all, are going to be able suddenly to turn around one day and believe singlemindedly in one love, committing themselves body and soul to building it forever? That having gotten used to using sex as a fun thing they are going to turn around and use it to express a totally committed, sacred relationship? I can't. I think habit, and particularly sexual habits, which affect us so deeply, are too strong for that. Statistics bear me out. A variety of sources indicate that those who fool around before marriage have trouble after marriage.

Christian Answers on Sex   35

Of course, it doesn't happen that way to everyone. There are many exceptions — people who, despite premarital sex, formed good marriages. But when you're dealing with something as important as this, doesn't it make sense to play the odds as much in your favor as you can?

I'm writing you because I obviously have a problem with sex. I am 15 and I'm in love with a guy of 17. We've been going together for one year and a month. In that time we have run into sex more than enough. To sum it all up, I love God but I also love my boyfriend. I don't want to hurt God because He's been very good to me, but at the same time there's my boyfriend. We're very close, and sex comes up quite often, and I can't say no. So what can I do to not offend either my boyfriend or God?

MAYBE THE BEST answer I can give is from another girl who wrote me:

▶ I want to emphasize the fact that you cannot have an honest relationship with God when you are indulging in premarital sex. In fact, I would venture to say that you can't have any relationship at all with God. It is like Jesus said, "No man can serve two masters."

I had dated this one guy for about six months before we decided to "go all the way." When I first met him I literally hated him, but after I got to know him better I started liking him and eventually grew to love him. During our sex relationship I accepted Jesus into my heart. However, because I was seeing this guy it didn't take long for me to get away from God. At first I had felt we should quit sex, but as Jesus said in Mark 7:38, "The spirit truly is ready, but the flesh is weak."

So we kept having our relationship and I got farther away from the Lord. Pretty soon it was like I was getting little warning signals from God saying, "Come back to Me. This isn't the way for you." But I kept on, and things got worse. This guy's feelings for me began to diminish; we saw less and less of each other; there were more noticeable signs of him using me. Finally after a great tragedy in my family — six people were killed — I turned and gave my life back to God, and this guy and I broke up.

That's one voice, and I am sure I could find others who would say sex hasn't hurt their relationship to God at all. But that doesn't make sense to me. God has made it quite clear He wants us to use the gift of sex only in the ideal setting of marriage. And how can you keep on ignoring what He says and maintain a good relationship with Him?

As for your boyfriend, I don't know how you can disregard what he wants and keep a good relationship with him, either. But if he wants sex more than a good relationship with you, how worthwhile is his love? Either you'll have to choose — or he'll have to change.

I have gone to bed with quite a few different girls, enjoyed it, and intend to make love to quite a few more. Why do people insist on making sex such a big deal? Sex is something different in every relationship. Sometimes there's a lot of personal emotion involved, and that's great. But other times it's just fun and exciting. Even if you tell each other you're in love, you both know it's not so serious. Why do people have to draw up rules that make something complex out of something very simple?

YOUR QUESTION OFFERS the *Playboy* philosophy. It suggests that having sex is like kissing, only more so. A kiss takes its meaning from the circumstances — when your aunt kisses you it means a different thing from a kiss under the moonlight. By the same token, why can't sex mean different things in different circumstances? Just because it's sometimes an act of total commitment, does that mean it always has to be? Why can't it sometimes just be for pleasure, when both partners want it and it isn't hurting anyone?

The answer is basic and hard to prove: *you don't understand sex. It isn't like that.* Sex is an act which affects us to the core, whether we like it or not.

To some extent you see that in the "Big Three": pregnancy, venereal disease, and guilt. I call them the Big Three because for years they were *the* reasons you were supposed to wait for marriage. Now they aren't so significant as arguing points, because with the Pill and abortion to deal with pregnancy, drugs to deal with VD, and a society that doesn't make you feel guilty for not "keeping pure," you can work around them. So if I argued that they were good reasons to keep from sex, anyone could answer with "What-if?" I believe premarital sex is a mistake whether someone gets pregnant or not.

But one thing we do learn from the Big Three: sex is a matter of life and death, literally.

Did you know that about a third of the girls who have premarital sex end up pregnant? No one ever got pregnant from kissing, but sex is an action which is serious enough to lead to the creation of a child. Then you're faced with one of four choices. You can rush into marriage — and the marriages usually are unhappy. You can have an abortion. You can give the child up for adoption. Or you can try to support the child yourself. Not one of these is an attractive option. Each one will drastically affect the life of three people: the father, the mother, and the baby.

My point isn't that this proves how awful it is to have sex before marriage. My point is that sex is biologically much more significant than a lingering kiss. It leads to the creation of human life.

And then there's VD. Despite the cures available, there is more VD than ever. It is curable, but many people never get treated. And it's not the only disease. The rate of cervical cancer is almost twice as high among girls who started having sex early — like before 16. So, in another biological way, sex proves more significant than a kiss. In fact, it's in a class all by itself. Is God trying to tell us something?

What about guilt? There aren't any statistics, but I can tell you that even in this liberated age people often are hounded by it. Many sad, guilty people have written me, and most of them say, "I never thought I would feel this way. If I had, I would never have gone ahead." Psychologically, sex proves to be a very complex subject.

Of course, at one level sex is simple. It's something we have in common with animals. Most of us will experience it in the course of our lives, and all the how-to manuals to the contrary, it comes quite naturally. Sex is also very demo-

A Love Story

cratic. A friend has pointed out how ironic this must have been in the Middle Ages, when life was far from democratic. A king had power then which no man has today. There were few limits to his whims, but there was one thing his power could never buy him: a better time in bed than the lowliest peasant in his kingdom. The peasants might gawk at the king's clothes, admire his castle, and dream of the rich food he ate while they survived on porridge, but in bed they lived as richly as he did.

But however democratic sex is, it remains extraordinary. Sexually we are not like animals. An animal's sexual relations are usually compulsive, as you know if you've ever had a dog in heat. But we humans can and do restrain our impulses; we have that power. What's more, we desire more than willingness in our partner. Most animals only want another animal to hold still. We humans make love face to face, gazing into each other's eyes; we need love, tenderness, and affection. That's built right into our biological nature, in the fact that men and women respond differently to sex, and to reach ideal sex have to communicate and help each other.

We are looking for something much deeper than a sexual experience. If we weren't, wouldn't prostitution be an attractive option?

Many people seem to think of sex as similar to Play-Doh, that bright-colored kid's clay. Play-Doh doesn't require much sophistication to use at maximum efficiency. It's just fun. Sometimes it's more fun than other times, depending on who you're playing with, but that doesn't make it very complex. If you're marketing Play-Doh, the main thing is distribution. Get it out to as many people as possible, and let them make up their own rules as to how to use it.

But marketing dynamite is different. You have to be careful about who buys it, and you have to encourage the buyer to use it carefully. You want to discourage amateur spontaneity, because dynamite is so powerful it can destroy things. You can move mountains with dynamite, but you also can blow yourself to pieces.

I think sex is more like dynamite than Play-Doh. Sex is powerful. More pleasure comes from sex than almost anything else, but more tears are shed because of it, too.

That doesn't mean sex is bad, or dirty. Is dynamite bad? No, it's just powerful. You have to focus it in specific ways in order for it to do any good. Otherwise, it either just makes an impressive noise, or actually ends up hurting you.

Sex is like that. Unfocused, it's still impressive stuff. It's more entertaining than Play-Doh any time. But it can also hurt you. And its ideal purpose goes far beyond playing around.

There's another way sex is like dynamite: staying power. Though Play-Doh is nice stuff, people usually get bored with it by the time they're eight. An adult who sees some Play-Doh lying out will hardly ever stop to play with it. But most adults still find dynamite intriguing.

Sex never gets boring, either. In fact, many people seem infatuated with it. Porno-flick theaters, singles pick-up bars, a million songs of love on the radio, any magazine rack, any beach, most TV commercials — they all testify to the incredible attraction of sex. If it's simple stuff, "just fun," why can't we act like it? The old answer was that people were so hung up by Victorian repression that their sexual instincts had turned perverse. But surely that argument is far out of date. We are no longer people with much of a Victorian hangover. Yet we still can't get over the marvel of sexuality.

That's because we're looking for more than "just sex." We are lonely people looking for loving unity with another person. We are never content with brief pleasures. We want to merge our lives with the lives of another. We look for the kind of relationship that will never leave us feeling alone again.

Sex is a part of that, which is why we become obsessed with it. But try to separate sex from deeply committed love, and you end up with an act that only apes what sex is meant to be.

Yes, it still feels good, done right or done wrong. And dynamite still makes a loud noise if you blow it off carelessly. But the end result isn't good.

I've had a chance to watch college friends who thought free sex was the way to go. They did enjoy sex. In talking to them I felt pretty foolish: what did I know? How could I defend my Christian ideas when they were so experienced?

But for most of them the long-term results have not been so wonderful. They do not seem so proud of being free with sex any more. Some of them seem, incredibly, a little bored with sex. A little tired. Perhaps a little sad. A parade of partners never satisfied them; it was always the next partner who would be perfect. Even those who eventually got married often were troubled by the discovery that their "perfect partner" wasn't so perfect; affairs or divorce followed.

And I also get letters. They don't prove anything statistically, but it is moving to get a letter from someone who had written before defending free sex, who now writes sadly to say how wrong he or she had been.

Sex is serious. It is an act in a category all its own. There is nothing really like it. If you want to understand it, you have to understand love, which is also both simple and extraordinarily complex. Love is an art. To create good art requires a combination of disciplined care and spontaneous creativity. And so does sex. Those who want to dabble won't become great artists. They will miss the fullness of sex.

T*wo kids in my church (I'll call them John and Marilyn) recently announced their wedding. They also told us, the other kids in the church, that Marilyn was pregnant.*

These two were very much looked up to by the younger kids — they are leaders. They told us they felt God has forgiven them, which is probably true, but I'm confused as to how God is going to look on their lives from here on out. Sure, He's forgiven their initial sin, but they're going to have a child out of that sin. How will He look upon that child? How can God bless Marilyn and John's union when it was forced on them by sin?

I have been talking to one friend about the church, but now I am embarrassed to invite her to come. What can she possibly think about the church when she finds out about Marilyn and John? No one keeps it a secret.

How should I react? Should I stand behind them, back them up? Should I stop trusting them? Is this a case where I can forgive and forget?

YOU CAN'T HAVE it both ways. Either God forgives or He doesn't. The forgiveness is total, according to the Bible — leaving no room for continuing guilt in those who are genuinely sorry and willing to change. The worst thing John and Marilyn could do now would be to doubt God's forgiveness and keep torturing themselves over their mistake.

This worries people, for obvious reasons. If you can be forgiven that easily, won't everyone starting sinning? Won't it set a poor example for other kids who are tempted? It's scandalous of God to let people off as though they hadn't done a thing. But that is exactly the scandal God is involved in. Apparently He's less concerned with making examples of people than He is with ending the rule of sin and guilt in human lives.

This forgiveness is the uniqueness of the Christian view of sex. Most religions (and cultures) have guidelines on sex; we're not unique in that respect. But our God offers forgiveness for mistakes.

You could, if you wanted, stop all outward sins by shackling people in chains. You can get almost the same effect by shackling them in fear and guilt. This is the way some Christians operate: they're so afraid of sin they make sure anyone who gets caught is ostracized and viewed with suspicion for a long time.

But God knows that the only difference between the sinners and those punishing them is that the sinners got caught. Everyone sins, even if they don't do it obviously. God is big enough to handle sins. By forgiving us when we come to Him, He hopes to convert us to a new way of life — happy obedience. His kind of people aren't coerced by fear and guilt into doing right. They do right out of gratefulness to Him.

So how will God look on John and Marilyn, and on their future child? With complete love. As far as He is concerned, it's as though they never sinned, but were a family formed in the most ideal way possible.

What about inviting a friend to the church, now that two of the leaders are fallen? I think many Christians are going to be asking that same question, because as our society's sexual morals get looser, more Christians are going to be tempted into the world's way. We shouldn't be shocked when it happens; we ought to be examples of forgiveness and love.

What would appeal most to a guest? Uptight people jealously guarding their perfection? Or a loving, forgiving community? Who do you like the most when you fail a test? Do you want to hang around the "A" students? No — you're interested in people who know what it feels like to fail, but whose life isn't shattered by the experience.

One thing I don't understand: how come God made us the way we are? Almost any good-looking girl makes me think about sex. Sexual attraction is there all the time, whether I want to think about it or not. But according to you God wants me to have sex with only one person. Why, then, did He make sex attractive with everyone, all the time? Did He want to make me miserable? Why couldn't He make it desirable only after you're married?

WE DON'T KNOW whether God could have made us that way or not. Ecologically, we've learned, His creation is finely balanced. Everything fits together, and changing one point without disturbing others may be impossible.

But suppose that God *could* have done it differently. Could there be a reason why He didn't?

I think so. I think that struggling to deal with our sexuality teaches us more about God than anything else. Letha Scanzoni has developed these ideas at length in her excellent book, *Why Wait?*

Sexually we're attracted to many people. Even when we're married, many people remain attractive. But to be really fulfilled, we have to train ourselves to put those other attractions aside, and focus on one person. We give up many sexual relationships in order to experience one totally loving relationship.

That's similar to our relationship with God. In the Bible His friendship with us is compared to a marriage — a marriage in which God is "jealous." He doesn't want to share us. He will not be put in second place to some idol: money, sex, sports, family. We must love Him with all our heart, soul, mind, and strength, as Jesus said.

This is hard to do. We don't like to choose. We want to have everything at once. But we can't. God must come first. Other things must be put aside.

You learn how to do this through your sexuality. Many people are attractive, yet each of us has to get beyond the phase where he falls in love with someone different every week. Ultimately we have to choose one person, and make the most of that relationship. Might it help to know that, in doing that, we're engaged in on-the-ground training for our relationship with God?

⇒ I think we can summarize the Christian point of view on sex this way: first, a sexual relationship is something important, complex, beautiful, difficult, and demanding. It takes in every part of us: spiritually, emotionally, mentally, and physically.

Second, God has given a wonderful framework for this difficult relationship: marriage. Marriage doesn't guarantee happiness, but it does contain the best conditions for making our love truly fulfilling.

It's odd, though, to talk about something so personal in a dry and theoretical way. I want to close this chapter by sharing some letters that have meant much to me. They are intensely personal. They don't "prove" anything. Each person's experience is different, the only common element being they all had sexual intercourse outside marriage and are sorry. At the least you can learn from them that sex hurts people badly if misused. Certainly that is the message they urgently want to get across.

▶ **I am 19 years old and single.** When I was in high school all the guys I hung around with were always talking about how far they went with their girl friends. At the time I had never gone all the way, and I thought I was missing something. But I was soon to find out that I wasn't missing a thing.

I'd been dating one girl steadily for four months, and we were doing some pretty heavy petting. But I would always find some excuse when it came to going all the way. I was brought

A Love Story

up in a very religious home, and had been taught that sex was meant for married people only.

But then I thought, after all, my parents didn't realize how much things had changed. So when my girl friend and I were out parking one night, I decided no matter what, I wasn't going to back out. I was going to go ahead and see what these other guys were talking about.

We had sex that night, and I still regret it to this day. I really thought I loved this girl, and we were thinking seriously about marriage. But after that I realized I didn't really love her so much as I thought. Soon we were bitter toward each other, and constantly arguing about everything.

I firmly believe that one night caused all our problems. Before long we broke off our relationship.

Now I am engaged to a different girl. Both of us feel the same way about sex before marriage. We are going to wait.

▶ **I recently broke up with a guy** I'd been going with for over a year. After we had gone together for about six months we went all the way. At that time, we had full intentions to marry sometime in the future. We thought of ourselves as responsible because we used birth control.

We did it a couple of times a month for a couple of months until one time we got too carried away and forgot about using birth control.

The next month was hell for me. I was so scared I was pregnant that the situation began to affect my grades, my nerves, and my disposition.

My relationship with this guy continued for a few months more until I finally tired of him and we broke up. This was really painful for me because of what we had done. Painful memories of this relationship haunt me now and these memories will probably not go away for a long time to come.

This is my real reason for writing — to tell those whose rationalization is "We're going to marry anyway, so why not?" that you may tire of the one you wish to have sex with, and breaking up will be a rough experience. After that, any new relationship will cause you pain because of your past. I dread the day when I will consider a relationship with some guy serious enough so that I will be forced to tell him.

▶ **As a sophomore in high school I had dated some,** but never had a steady boyfriend. Then in January I met a guy I really liked (perhaps even loved). In May he broke up with me because he had a fiancee in another town. A year later I was still not over the hurt and shock. I was determined never to go through that pain again. I dated other guys that year, but I wouldn't let myself become involved.

Then this January (as a junior) I earnestly prayed that God would send me someone whom I could love and who would love me in return. I wanted a Christian and I believed God would answer my prayer. On January 20 my church had a rally and I was introduced to a very nice-looking Christian guy of my own denomination . We hit it off beautifully and often remarked how God had brought us together — for he had prayed as I had.

About a month later John gave me his class ring. It was love and we both realized it. There were not enough hours in the day for us to see each other. Our love grew and grew. Then John, a very ambitious guy, decided to open his own business in the town where I live. He had just turned 18 and was still a senior in high school, so opening a donut shop put quite a strain on us. We sacrificed our dating time to work in the shop. Everything we did or talked about revolved around it. Since he had a place of his own, we started going there on dates. It was innocent enough to start with. We kissed and he would touch my breasts. Then we started undressing and going to bed. After this had gone on for a while, he gave me a promise ring. The ring only made us go farther in our sexual desires.

Shortly after John gave me the ring, I began to notice that his ambition had turned to greed. He wasn't satisfied with one shop; he wanted two. He wanted a nicer car, a better place to live. I watched him change from his old self into a greedy human monster.

In May, I decided to go away to summer school for five weeks. I planned to come home every weekend, and write and call. A week after the school accepted me he broke up with me. The only reason he gave was that he didn't love me any more.

I was deeply hurt. I loved him so desperately I couldn't stand the thought of losing him. I was jealous of other girls. I tried everything to get him back — phone calls, letters, etc.

I went away to school and would come back home, broken-hearted, weekend after weekend. John began telling me that everything we ever had was over. He said he wasn't even sure if he ever really loved me. I felt so cheap then because I remembered all the times I had gone to bed with him.

A Love Story

Then I thought that if John didn't love me I must not be worth much. So while I was away at school, I slept with another guy.

I realized I was wrong for doing that because it reminded me so painfully of the times I'd spent with John. I also knew it was wrong in the sight of God. I prayed for forgiveness and since then I haven't even gone out with anyone else. I know that God has forgiven me, but I still feel guilty — and I feel regret.

I returned home at the end of five weeks to find John completely changed. He was dating the wildest girls around, trying to see how many he could date in a week. He changed to another church. He had lost pride in his business. He still walks around with dollar signs in his eyes and he wants to be very rich, but he is spending his money very foolishly and his business is going downhill.

We had a long talk and decided to be friends. It's hard for me to watch him ruin his life as he is. I know I still love him and I am constantly worried about him and the shop. He has scores of "friends" now who are wild about his money and apartment — not him. But he can't see that.

Today, I went to his shop to return something to him. We started talking. He told me that he was confused, but that his friends were a great comfort to him. I lightly hinted that he might be running away from his problems, but he told me to not preach to him.

John tells everyone how much he doesn't care for me, but if I don't see him for about a week, he'll just happen to walk by or something. To me he is screaming that he needs someone. He is constantly trying to shock me by telling me about his love life. Today he was telling me how many hickeys he had given this girl — and I became sick — *really sick* of him.

Before, I pitied him because he was confused and was shutting God out of his life. Even though I knew he no longer loved me, I prayed constantly for him. I prayed that he wouldn't lose his business, because it's all he has. But today I looked at him and saw that he acted about four years old. I felt old, like I had grown up very quickly and he had never grown at all. I no longer felt love or pity, but rather a twinge of hatred began to grow. Now I pray that he will lose his business because I feel that is the only way God can humble him.

It hurts me to see him this way. Today I wished that I would never have to see him again — or better yet, that I had never met him. I want to get through my senior year as quickly as possible and leave him and this town.

I am deeply scarred because I was not strong enough to

say no to him. How do I ever get over the guilt? More important, though — how do I stop loving and caring? At one time we both felt our relationship was God's will. At times I still hear a voice in my heart that whispers, "It will work out in three years." But what until then? I wholeheartedly believe that John and I were "meant to be." I have never felt such a consuming love for anyone and it seems the more he tries to hurt me, the more love I have for him. Does this love come from God?

I'm desperate. How do I make it through another year of school? Although he's not in school, he has dated almost every girl who is available. I feel awkward around them now.

Please help me. I want to be loved again, but not hurt.

▶ **Like everyone else** I'll start my letter with some background information about myself. I am 18 years old and my boyfriend is 21. We have been dating about three-and-a-half years. About eight months after we started dating we started participating in sex. I'm not talking about intercourse, only everything else. But that really doesn't matter because I now feel that sex is sex and the little sex actions make you feel just as bad as the "big one" (intercourse).

I hear from all the "older" folks that you cannot control your emotions and that sooner or later you will get "carried away." I don't believe this is true. I feel that you can control your emotions and urges — but I also believe you won't want to.

My boyfriend and I only had intercourse after we had been dating three years. Both of us have been brought up in Christian homes and I think this had a great deal to do with our putting it off and off and off. . . .

At one time we were both very close to God and had a good relationship with Him. I guess the whole point of my letter is to say this: slowly our indulgence with sex interfered with our relationship with our Lord. The feelings of guilt have always been there, and that is why I know premarital sex is wrong, but I can only talk for myself. I have tried to put aside my guilt and convince myself that it is okay, but I can't. We both fell away from God, not even noticing it until it got to the point where we were very far from Him. I still attend church every Sunday, but I have no/very little communication with God, because I replaced Him with another god — sex.

If I had seen what sex was going to do to us I never would have started. It didn't matter what people tried to tell me; I had to

A Love Story

find out for myself. Many times we have tried to give up our habit — but have failed. I find both good and bad in premarital sex. I also find that the bad outweighs the good, and therefore does not allow me to enjoy the good.

I wish no one would have the feelings that I have had in my relationship, although I'm sure many have. It takes away from something that is supposed to be sacred and beautiful — love. I hope this letter can point in the right direction someone who has mixed feelings about sex.

▶ **I fell in love with a girl** two years ago. We dated a few weeks before any real talk of sex entered our relationship. Both of us were very open and honest with each other about sex. We spent the rest of that spring and the following summer "experimenting." Before entering college that fall we both decided to have sex. We did. Our relationship began to lose something from then on. We tried sex again to make up for the loss but God's gift of sex became empty and sickeningly automatic, unreal. After almost five months of anxiety, pain, and deep frustration we broke up.

I accepted Jesus Christ as my Lord and Savior a year later and He healed a very bitter and torn soul. I still love this girl, and I tried to undo the hurt we did each other. My having sex with her weakened my witness about Christ to her.

It's been over a year now since the months of anguish and hell. Even with the forgiveness and love of Jesus I am still hurt and scarred inside. Jesus heals the pain and gives me the genuine sense of forgiveness, but the memories remain.

Fornication is a deeply personal kind of sin. It involves your very being: mind, body, heart, and soul. Paul wrote in 1 Corinthians 6:18, "Run from sex sin. No other sin affects the body as this one does. When you sin this sin it is against your own body" (LIVING BIBLE). I know exactly what Paul meant. I hope this letter will help someone to not make my mistake.

2

Pressure: How Far Do We Go?

It would be odd indeed if the Creator put attractive people in the world and forbade us to notice them.

Lewis Smedes, *Sex for Christians*

TWO COLLEGE STUDENTS from Texas wrote me. Their letter had touches of anger and rebellion, but the questions were good. They had much doubt about whether premarital sex was really wrong. But at the end of their letter they got down to what I suspect was really bothering them. In case you're someone who still thinks only guys are driven by sexual desires, let me mention that these students are both female. Here's what they wrote:

▶ **Suppose it has been established** without a doubt that sex before marriage is wrong. Again we cry out: WHAT DOES GOD EXPECT US TO DO IN THE MEANTIME? What about our sexual drives between now and our marriage? You may say, "Well, you must divert your attention to other things, draw up a 'plan,' pray, etc., etc." But sex is not something you put aside. It is not something you try to ignore. It is not just a desire. It is a *need!* Like hunger. The more you try to ignore it the worse it gets. We cannot just "wait." Please don't say that these desires should go away and we should try to suppress them and fix our thoughts on what is pure and good and lovely.

One young man spoke for many when he said: "The *Playboy* philosophy is not just a worldly rationalization for lust. It is rather the source of intense meaning for thousands . . . and if people don't understand the intensity of the problem of loneliness, they have no business moralizing on one of the most meaningful solutions young people have found. Quite frankly, we as Christians are not in much of a condition to condemn premarital sex if we have nothing better to offer the single person to answer his basic innate need."

Christians say the right way to handle sex is clear-cut: wait until marriage. Naturally, we know that there is a lot of difference between someone using sex (and other people) just for kicks and someone who feels deeply in love and expresses that love through sexual intercourse. Still, we put those cases in the same category. They blew it. They should have waited. No matter how great the pressure on them, and how worthy their motives, they shouldn't have gone all the way.

That is a very strict, and for many, unreasonable standard. It seems to some to be impossible. It seems like starving a dog for a week, and then putting a juicy bone in front of him while telling him to "stay." It's not only cruel, it's unworkable.

But does it have to work like that? I don't think so. Christian standards don't eliminate all frustration — nothing this side of heaven will. But they're meant to fulfill, not frustrate us.

Sex doesn't turn from bad to good the day you're married. I'm a sexual person. You're a sexual person. Everything you do has sexual overtones. The Bible reports that in the beginning God made Man male and female. We have sexual feelings, sexual drives. But those aren't necessarily hooked up to sexual intercourse. We can be fully sexual, but not be overwhelmed by frustration. Exhibit A is Jesus Christ, who experienced the same kinds of temptations we do, who was fully a man, sex drive and all, yet remained single all his life. He doesn't strike me as a hopelessly frustrated man.

Exhibit B are all the men and women, myself included, who don't go all the way yet fully enjoy being men and women. That enjoyment includes sexual urges and excitement.

Sex is a drive, not a need. A need is a gaping mouth that must be filled. A drive is in need of a steering wheel.

The two girls who wrote compared their sexual "needs" to hunger. But it's a poor analogy. There are two parts to hunger — a need and a desire. We *need* food to survive. We don't *need* sex. It won't make you sick to skip it.

But hunger is more than a need; it's also a desire or a drive. We like to eat. Food tastes good. A good meal satisfies more than the need for calories.

Sex *is* like this part of hunger. Intercourse is something we crave, even though we don't need it.

But everyone knows this kind of hunger should be controlled. You can't eat candy all day: from the time you were a small child your parents worked hard to teach you to eat what was really good for you. If you always ate what you felt like eating you'd be fat and unhealthy.

The same is true of sex. Our appetite needs to be con-

A Love Story

trolled for our own good. Sex is wonderful, but if we don't control it, it controls us.

Another analogy suggests that the sex drive is like steam under pressure. According to this, every time something stimulates you sexually a little more steam goes into your tank. It keeps building and bulding until it has to let go.

I just don't believe sex works like that. My experience is that if you put temptation aside, it doesn't come back stronger each time. The best way to make it come back stronger is to give in. From what I've seen, someone who normally engages in sex is often the most conscious of it, and is driven by it as a day-to-day need. The restrained person often worries about it the least. Sex builds on itself.

I don't mean you can cut out all the tension. You can't. You shouldn't. It's part of being human, and a good sign of maturity is the ability to handle tension creatively. That's also a good sign of a mature relationship.

Christianity does have a special answer for dealing with pressure. Did you notice how the letter from those two girls ended? They quoted from a guy who said Christians had better have an answer to the problem. But what was the problem, as he put it? Not sex. It was loneliness.

Most of what passes for a desire for sex is really a desire for intimacy. The one desire is easily mistaken for the other, because sex seems to bring intimacy so beautifully and easily. You really feel close, closer than you will ever feel to any other person.

I have reason to believe, however, that those good feelings often are phony. They tell lies. What feels like the greatest expression of mutual love may in fact be mostly an expression of mutual lust. If it is, it'll show eventually.

When I say Christians have a special answer for dealing with pressure, I am not talking about a supernatural power that will intervene and make you not want sex so badly. Nor am I thinking of a heavenly hand that will snatch you back from the brink. That may happen, but generally I think God prefers that we learn to deal with temptation, using the character we've developed in Him.

But He does offer something special: a cure to loneliness. He offers two ways of dealing with loneliness, really: Himself, and other Christians. That may seem rather far removed from a desire for sex, but I'm convinced it helps. It really helps me. I'm not driven by sex because I'm not driven by loneliness. Deep fellowship with God and with Christian friends makes me feel secure just the way I am.

I said "cure." I don't really mean that. Loneliness is part of life, and you don't ever lose it. You don't if you sleep with someone. You don't if you get married. It's always there: a dark cry for love. I think it's really a sense of incompleteness, a searching for God which is meant to keep us from getting too content and cocksure with life the way we live it. God doesn't cure that on this earth. I don't think He wants to.

But we often fasten that loneliness on one person, and think that our frustrations could be cured by going farther with him or her. They can't. Even the totally committed love and sex of marriage doesn't cure our frustrations. It takes God, plus many persons. Someday, unless what God says is all lies, we will experience the fullness our loneliness promises us. In the meantime, controlling our desires for sexual intimacy will always, for every healthy person, be a problem.

A girl lives about one hour from where I live. We have a really open, Christian relationship. We can talk to each other and tell what we feel without holding back any ideas or thoughts. We talk on the phone and write. We don't get to see each other a lot, and when we do, I always want to touch her. I think she feels the same way, because she wants to be alone with me a lot. I can control myself but sometimes it is awfully difficult. We don't know what's right. What in the Bible is there about the do's and don'ts of sex?

OUTSIDE OF THE warning against intercourse outside marriage, there isn't much. There isn't a word about how far to go, or whether petting is right or wrong. That's not surprising: in the time when the Bible was written, the sexes hardly saw each other before marriage. They certainly didn't get much opportunity to caress each other's bodies.

Petting gets defined many different ways. I'm talking

A Love Story

about caressing breasts or genitals. Even within that definition there's much variety: a guy who touches his girl friend's breasts through her clothes is in a different state than a couple lying together naked, doing everything but the act of intercourse. But the Bible doesn't speak of any of this. Nor does it mention holding hands, kissing, hugging, French kissing, or caressing. All of this is gray area. There are no specific biblical guidelines for Christians.

But people want guidelines. They want to know exactly how far they can go without sinning. I sympathize; I've felt that same way. But there isn't any answer. There really couldn't be: it's different with every relationship. Some relationships are casual: it's ridiculous to spend time making out. To do so would be simply to use each other.

Also, people react differently to things. What's unbearably sexy to one person may be rather mild to another. And this is especially true between guys and girls. A girl may simply get a pleasant feeling from, say, a guy touching her breasts. But her partner may be going wild with desire.

So I can't give any do's and don'ts. There is no magic line for how far you can go.

But then, isn't that question mixed up anyway? What people really want, I think, is a line so that they can go racing right up to it, dangling over the edge, as close as possible to tipping over.

The right question isn't "How far *can* we go?" but "How far *should* we go?" What actions are really helpful in expressing the love and commitment we feel for each other?

Most of us aren't great poets who can express love exactly the way we want to. We end up muttering monosyllables we know sound corny. But our love isn't corny, so we have to express it another way. Intercourse is the ultimate word: it says all there is to say about a committed relationship between the sexes.

Kissing, hugging, and petting are attempts to say something less than that. They're saying in their own unique way, "Here's how much I love you and care for you. It could be more, but this is where it's at right now."

So the question isn't really "How far?" but "What really says honestly where we're at?"

Let me put in a purely personal note at this point. For me, kissing expresses love as well as any action short of intercourse can. Any time I've gotten beyond kissing, I've ended up feeling hot and frustrated. I've felt as though I'd started something I couldn't finish. And torn between the pure sexual desire to go on, and my own responsibility to hold back, I wasn't thinking much about love. At that point it was sex, and the girl could have been any girl. Ending an evening feeling sweaty and unfulfilled is not my picture of the ideal. What good did it do? So for me the line is anything beyond a lengthy kiss.

But that's me. Some people I respect claim petting can be an innocent way of exploring a relationship, if it's done with integrity and love, not lust. All I know is that it doesn't seem to work that way for me. And I doubt it does for very many people.

Of course, that leaves a million unanswered questions. What about French kissing? Can we lie down together to kiss? Is it all right to caress anything but the breasts and genitals? You'll have to find the answers for yourself. But ask yourself: what do we want to say? And how far do we have to go to say it? I hope I don't need to say that you ought to ask yourself that *before* you're hot and heavy in each other's arms. Draw definite guidelines for yourself ahead of time: how far do I want to go? How *long* do I want to go? (That's one question seldom asked. But being plastered against each other for a half hour or so is a good deal different from a brief good-night kiss. The temptation to go farther is a lot stronger.) Set time limits, at least approximately, and when it's gone on long enough (you've said what you want to say), stand up and change the activity. Don't just separate by a few inches and expect things to cool off. Sex is not inert — once it gets going it takes specific actions to change its course.

Which brings up another point. Petting is not dirty. You may decide, as I have, that it's wrong for you. But don't forget that it's meant to be a beautiful thing in marriage, a natural expression leading up to sex.

The trouble is that petting is meant to move on to something more. By itself, it doesn't satisfy. The same is true all along the line: holding hands, hugging and kissing also arouse you. They point you to bigger pleasures.

You have to cope with this dynamic. First, it means there has to be restraint. You can't "try things out." The further you've gone, the more difficult it is to go back. If you've decided to kiss, you won't be satisfied to return to holding hands. If you've tried petting, cutting it out will be very hard. Our bodies are designed to take us onward.

Second, if you're going to hold the line you'll have to work at making your expressions meaningful. Take a kiss. At first it's wonderful. But if you're just thinking about the sexual pleasure, it'll become boring. Your body wants to go further. A kiss can become about as exciting as kissing your grandmother is.

But it doesn't have to be like that. If you concentrate on expressing love — on what you're putting into the kiss, not what you're getting out of it — it will stay a meaningful expression. Even married couples have to work at this, whether in their sex life, or in the kiss they give each other in the morning. Almost any action can become ritualized and meaningless, but that doesn't mean it has to. A meaning for a particular thing isn't strictly a function of the thrill it gives you. Praying, for instance, isn't always emotionally thrilling. Yet it is a symbol and means for communicating with God — something we have to keep working at.

One other thing. It's not enough to make up your mind about what's right for you. Sex comes only in pairs. You have another person's opinion to consider.

Seldom are two people at exactly the same point of commitment at the same time. One person may want to express much more love than the other (and he or she may get pretty pushy about it). Also, what means one thing to one person may mean something else to the partner: a kiss is like a handshake to some, but a deeply meaningful gesture to others.

I believe that you should never express physically more than either person is ready for. In other words, if your girl friend wants to pull you on top of her, but you don't feel right about that, don't do it. Don't just resist: talk and explain why. And don't give in.

On the other hand, if you feel much more outgoing than

your partner, don't sit around arguing with him or her about how it's not a sin and won't hurt anyone. So what if it won't? You're not trying to do something to see if you can get away with it: you're trying to express love. If your partner doesn't feel quite the way you do, make the sacrifice and express it at his or her level. What kind of love is it that won't?

Is petting harmful? I know it isn't going to give me a disease or grow hair on my palms, but can it cause harm? The reason I ask is that my boyfriend says it won't but sometimes I feel guilty afterward.

WHETHER IT WILL harm either of you, or hurt your relationship, I don't know. But it certainly can.

For one thing, petting can have the emotional effects intercourse does, though on a lower scale. It can arouse guilt or other powerful emotions that make you feel strange together. It can certainly interfere with the time you need to spend talking, so that you spend all your hours making out and your relationship becomes superficial.

It can, as it has for many people, be the bridge to intercourse. It is sexually exciting, sometimes beyond what you expect. There are many couples who found they reached a point where they simply had to go on; they couldn't stop. That point is different for each couple (and each occasion, too; because you were able to stop one week doesn't guarantee you'll be able to the next week).

Perhaps because of guilt feelings, petting has the potential to mess you up sexually. Psychologists and doctors don't understand why, but there's no question that many women who can't respond freely sexually in marriage — who are frigid — trace the feelings back to some early petting experiences. Some of them say that they got so used to responding to petting, and to the guarded self-control they needed to keep from going all the way, that they couldn't later abandon themselves to intercourse.

There is even, in heavy petting to climax, a slight chance

60   *A Love Story*

of pregnancy. If semen comes into contact with the vagina it will sometimes enter and, despite "virginity," pregnancy results. It seems rather humorous and improbable, but it does happen. When it does, it doesn't seem funny at all.

But the biggest danger, to me, is provoking all that unnecessary frustration. What good does it do? Dealing with frustration when you have to can, of course, be a growing experience, but that doesn't mean you try to invent troubles. Especially if you feel guilty, I'd say cut it out.

My boyfriend and I have been dating for seven months. He's 17 and I'm 16. I've never been the aggressive type, but from the beginning my boyfriend has been. First it was heavy kissing, then he put his hands under my blouse and finally . . . well, he's kept going. I told him I didn't want him to go that far again. He said OK, because he didn't want to do anything I didn't want him to. But now he's gone back to it. I try to make him stop, but he won't. He gets me on the couch and he gets on top of me and I can't get him off. Whenever I kiss him, he thinks I want him to start handling me. I don't want to break up with him because I really like him. If he would just control himself, he would be fine. What should I do?

MAKE IT VERY clear to Romeo that you mean business. Tell him you are through with him unless he cuts it out, for good. He's probably bought the old line that girls really want to, but they also want to be coaxed into it. If so, the only thing that will help him escape his illusions is your putting some force behind your words.

And if he won't respond to that, do just what you said: break it off. That sounds harsh, especially when you like every part of his personality except this one. But the trouble is, you can't split up a personality. If he won't control himself in this, he won't control himself in other things. If he won't be unselfish here, he'll be selfish all the way down the line. As hard as it seems, the relationship ought to be severed: it would be going nowhere.

I *have been dating Karen for seven months, and we have had a*
beautiful, fantastic relationship. I told her when I first started to
take her out that I didn't want to get involved in premarital sex.
She agreed. You have to understand what kind of girl she is —
sweet and very innocent. I love her very much and I know she
loves me.

On New Year's Eve she came over to my house. She was up
in my room looking it over and we just started to neck on my bed.
She had on a low-neck dress and before I knew it I was in it. After
we realized what we had done, we both told each other we were
sorry, but then she told me that she wasn't. We both agreed that
we enjoyed it and that it made us love each other all the more. We
both said that we wouldn't do it again. Can you explain this
situation to us? Do you think that it happened for a certain
purpose? Do you think that God made it happen? I have never
done this kind of thing before and it really has us both down.

SOME PEOPLE WOULD find it humorous that a sweet, innocent girl who just happened to be in a low-cut dress happened to be in her boyfriend's bedroom where they "just
started to neck," and where "before he knew it" he was
inside her dress. But if I laugh, I'm also laughing at myself.
Often enough I've found myself doing things I hadn't
planned on. Yet looking back, I also see that subconsciously I
had been making preparations all along. It leaves me feeling a
little like a hunter, caught in a noose which swoops him off
his feet upside-down. As blood rushes to his head and he
dangles helplessly, he remembers that he set the trap himself
last week.

Couples play these games too much: they just happen to
be in an empty house, and then without warning they find
themselves making out, and then, to their surprise, they find
themselves going further than they'd planned. Considering
the physical exertion and teamwork required, it's astonishing how many couples go too far "by accident."

So did God make it happen? You could make a far better

A Love Story

case that you two made it happen — with a dose of help from an active, normal sex drive.

The interesting part is your surprise that you enjoyed it, and that it "made us love each other all the more." (By that last phrase I presume you mean you felt closer to each other — that the emotions were warm.) But what could you expect? God made sex for, among other things, pleasure and the expression of love. There is no "on/off" switch activating this the day you get married. Sex feels good anytime. It should always give you warm, intimate feelings. If that weren't true, I don't think it would be any problem for people to stick with the biblical idea of waiting for marriage. As a matter of fact, many people experience sex and have the same reaction you did: "Hey, that's not so bad! In fact, it's wonderful! All those puritans must have been keeping this thing off limits because they didn't want me to enjoy myself."

The reason some kinds of sexual expression ought to be kept in marriage isn't because they don't feel good outside of marriage. It's that they are too big for anything less than the quality of relationship you find in a committed, loving, Christian marriage.

God seemed to match my boyfriend and me. We often talk about God, pray together and share our deepest and innermost feelings. We love each other very much, and plan to be married in about four years.

For a long time we were very careful not to have any sexual contact except for kissing. But as time wore on, our needs and desires grew and grew. Once or twice we'd slip, but then we'd talk about it, set our limits and go from there. We went through a long period of doubts and confusion, praying and listening to God, searching the Bible and discussing. Because the Bible definitely forbids fornication, we decided never to go all the way.

But the Bible doesn't state clearly where the line is. Our final conclusion was this: as long as it doesn't hurt our relationship in any way, and as long as God placed no feelings of guilt in either of us, anything was allowed except going all the way. There were conditions: only when we have plenty of time, thus not causing us to get in late; only when we are sure there will be no interruption; and only after a lengthy period of time has elapsed since the last time we indulged.

In petting each other to a climax, we have experienced great joy in each other. I cannot see any way in which it has hurt our relationship to God or to one another. If anything, I think it has strengthened our relationship.

What is your opinion and advice concerning us? Is petting to a climax really immoral, or is it the penis entering the vagina that is wrong? True, petting of any kind would be wrong if it hurts a relationship — and I know it often does. But does it hold true to our situation? If we are wrong, we would be willing to quit, simply to please God. But neither of us has felt any evidence that God is displeased. Before, lust would sometimes block God out of our minds. But now, because of satisfaction, we feel closer to Him.

THIS QUESTION PROBES a gray area of the Bible acutely. The Bible doesn't state where the line is, and opinions about petting or even about kissing are only interpretations of biblical principles. Your letter describes the ultimate case to be made in favor of petting to a climax. Few couples could honestly claim the same loving, prayerful searching in their relationship.

Of course, nearly all the objections normally raised to petting would apply, except for the frustration petting normally brings: by petting to climax you eliminate that frustration.

But I still think it's wrong. Let me make it clear that this is my opinion. It's not what the Bible says; it's how I understand the Bible. And others may differ. See if this makes sense to you.

Your ideas, it seems to me, make virginity into a technicality, a membrane either punctured or unpunctured. I don't believe God's concern for virginity outside marriage relates to that membrane. I think it relates to intercourse's total intimacy, the "nakedness" physically and emotionally which sex ideally represents. Petting to climax is short of intercourse in terms of its pleasure and emotion, but it seems to me that it does have that total "nakedness." There is almost

A Love Story

nothing held back. This isn't simply an expression of love, as a kiss is, but an almost unreserved plunging into union. If that's so, then I believe that kind of sexual intimacy is reserved for marriage. It's only technically (and less satisfyingly) different from intercourse. That's where the phrase "technical virgin" came from.

Incidentally, Christ's remarks about "looking at a woman with lust" being a form of adultery points us in this same direction. It's the mental operation, not a physical action, that Christ finds fault with. In petting to climax, I think the mental and spiritual nakedness between you is more significant than the position you're in when you stimulate each other genitally.

And what is the reason for petting to climax? Basically, you're dealing with the frustrations of your sexual drives. I can sympathize with that. It is very hard to wait, and the closer you become to each other, the more you desire the complete intimacy of sexual intercourse. Our society, by making marriage a strictly adult thing, intensifies the pressure.

What's the answer? In some cases, it may be to make sacrifices and get married. If you're too young for that, perhaps you're also too young for the all-out intimacy of being "practically married" for years. Perhaps you should cool it for a while. Your relationship, if it's right, won't be damaged by giving each other some time and space to grow in.

But if those aren't possible solutions, your only choice is to wait — and struggle. There is one consolation: learning to wait can do you a great deal of good. Marriage is a hard business in our society — much harder than in times and places where its permanency wasn't threatened by social forces. It could be that learning to control strong sexual drives before marriage is just the training you need to control other deep, dangerous forces you'll confront — forces like greed, selfishness, and jealousy. Could waiting be a training session God wants you to experience?

I*'ve been dating a new Christian. In fact, I'd dated him before he became a Christian. When the relationship led to petting I couldn't control the situation. I prayed a lot and finally decided to break it off.*

Now, some time later, we're back together. I had decided to cut off the sex completely except for a good-night kiss, but it didn't work. We've talked of marriage: I'm out of school now, but if we're not mature enough to handle sex, I can't see how we'd handle marriage. Now when I'm with him I don't care what we do. The only time I feel bad is afterward, when I realize it's wrong and I should have enough love for God to do what's right.

This summer I've felt depressed and alone. Seeing him is all I live for. I try to do what's right. I pray, but then I hate myself. I have only one person to talk to. Please tell me what to do. I'm going crazy.

YOURS IS A common discovery: that sexual intimacy has powerful momentum. It can affect you more powerfully than you expect. That's why some people who've gotten involved in sex warn others away by saying things like, "Sex is addictive. Once you start you can't stop." Corny as that sounds, there's some truth in it. Beforehand, you tend to think sex is something you can handle — it's just an action. Afterward, however, you discover there are all kinds of strings attached. In marriage those strings make sense — they fit the total commitment of the relationship. But outside marriage they tend to mess you up.

So in a case like this, it *will* be difficult to straighten things out. Powerful forces have been unleashed. You are right not to jump into marriage. Guilt and frustration aren't good motives to begin marriage with, and statements like "seeing him is all I live for" indicate your relationship isn't very well balanced. It wouldn't be too long after marriage before you would realize he isn't enough to live for. Then you'd feel more trapped than you do now.

It struck me that you never mentioned what your boyfriend thinks about all this. Could you have left that out by accident? I'll bet you haven't honestly discussed things (not just sex, but your whole relationship). Until you do, there's

A Love Story

little or no hope. Even with two agreeing to work on controlling sex, it's very difficult. If two people can't agree on this, and can't work together, then they ought to break it off. The relationship isn't going anywhere.

But there is hope for change, as long as there's a genuine friendship to work together for it. I'd like to quote from one letter I got:

▶ **In a recent issue you told** two Christian kids to be creative in their relationship, so not so much "free time" is left open. I just wanted to share what my fiancé and I have discovered in this area of our relationship.

We both feel premarital sex is wrong. But . . . where to draw the line was becoming more and more difficult. We both were feeling mighty guilty and often said, "We've got to quit." Finally at Christmastime God really put the thumb on us, and we came before Him and asked for His help — His power. It was like a ten-ton burden was lifted! We set limits: no lying down, no petting at all. We tried to think of ways to be creative in expressing our love. We're still learning, but here are a few ways we've found bring intense satisfaction — much more than we've ever found from frustrated and unfulfilled physical expression.

1. He gave me a rose for no special reason.
2. We've written poems for each other. We've also just shared classical poetry, love poems by the great poets. Sometimes they say what you're feeling, but could never express.
3. We sing to each other.
4. We shop together. Any couple that can shop for four hours together without getting irritable has definitely learned a lesson in getting along.
5. We work on hobbies together.
6. We spend time with other couples.
7. And the most exciting thing we've found is praying for each other.

Sharing in other ways now will make our sexual relationship after marriage so much more precious. Before God turned us around, I'd never thought much about an actual sexual experience — just kind of got carried away in "how good it felt" to pet. I never wanted the real thing — I was scared. Now I'm anxiously waiting for sex. God has changed so many attitudes since we surrendered to Him.

I know now that if you really want to love a person you have to be willing to be a bit frustrated at times, and come up with a creative alternative in order to be in a place where God can pour out His blessing in full on the relationship.

I like this letter particularly because it shows that controlling sex doesn't mean you turn it off and become sterile. The writer claims more appreciation and anticipation of sex — not less.

One other important thing for those in this position: please realize God wants to forgive you. You aren't helping anything by hating yourself — in fact, the guilt feelings probably drive you steadily into more failure. And God isn't happy to see you hating yourself.

Everyone fails, and nearly everyone experiences guilt at some point in life. The incredible, marvelous thing about being a Christian is that we have forgiveness. There are no strings attached . . . you cannot sin more times than God will forgive you. If you can find the joy and beauty of that forgiveness, I think it will help you deal with your problem. Most misuses of sex come as a result of reaching out for love. God's loving will help fill that void in your life — and reduce the motive that drives you back into something you don't want to do.

Talking to a pastor or a strong, older Christian can be a great help in experiencing this forgiveness. Hearing someone say, "I forgive you and God forgives you" puts flesh and blood to what you know in your head. I'd recommend you go to such a person and ask point-blank, "Do you forgive me? Does God?" You need to hear the audible answer: "Yes. I do. He does. You are forgiven."

You have written how wrong premarital intercourse is, why God doesn't approve of it, and how it can cause problems. I agree with you on all these things. But tell me this: how do I stop?

My fiance and I want to please God, but it seems like we just can't stop having sex. There are many reasons – I come from a broken home (I am in a foster home), and before I was saved I would use sex as an escape from my problems. I know it is no excuse, but maybe it explains how we started having this problem in the first place. For a long time I tried to say no, but the last couple of months I have been getting so discouraged, I don't even *try. I want to stop more than anything, but I don't know how. Deep down, my fiancé doesn't really want to stop. He wants to please God, but it's hard for him to give up sex.*

We've both prayed about this for a long time, together and separately, but we just don't seem to get anywhere.

TRYING HARD NOT to want sex is like trying not to think of pink elephants — the harder you try, the more you fail. So if you're in this situation, forget any idea of not *wanting* sex. You're looking for self-control — more or less the same kind of control it takes to lose weight, or to study for a test when you don't feel like it.

I'm going to suggest a plan — not the only plan possible, but one I think has a good chance of working. You need something concrete — and if you both can't agree on a good plan, or if you agree but then don't work at it, I'd guess not only is the plan doomed, but your relationship would seem likely to end unhappily also.

Take a moment to analyze what's going on. The problem isn't totally different from trying to control, say, urges to pet. You're experiencing what some people refer to as the "addiction" of sex. Once you've gone so far, it's hard to stop — and almost impossible to go back. Intercourse is something like the starburst at the end of the trip, and it's especially powerful. Once its power is awakened in your relationship, it's hard to put it back to sleep.

This is a wonderful thing, designed by God. When marriage works in the ideal way, everything pulls in its favor — even the human body. It's wonderful that intercourse can pull a married couple back together time after time.

For unmarried people, sex is cruelly hard to stop while still continuing the relationship. It's so difficult, in fact, that some suggest you just go on doing it. I don't agree. That sounds like saying that once Jack of "Jack and the Beanstalk" has wakened the giant, he might as well give up and be his slave. It's possible, though difficult, to put the giant back to sleep. And in the long run learning to control yourselves, to forgive and make a new beginning, might build your relationship at just the points where it badly needs strengthening.

Christian Answers on Sex 69

Once you've awakened the giant, you can't pretend he's not there. That's the mistake most couples make in dealing with this: they try to control sex by ignoring it. But sex is too big and too powerful for that. You can't ignore it. You can't just "go on with your relationship." You have to stop things and get them in order before you can "go on" with anything.

I think that involves penalties — not punishments, as though suffering in itself will make up for mistakes. Just penalties — payment for repairs. Don't expect to stop without giving some things up.

But before doing anything else, make sure you are forgiven by God. Read 1 John 1:9 and get it inside your head. It's funny how some people try to hold on to their guilt, thinking that if they concentrate on how awful they are they'll somehow stop acting awful. Actually, guilt just drives you back to the same sin — if you're worthless, why not at least get a little solace from sex? If you know how strongly God loves you, and how idealistically He sees you, you'll want to act accordingly.

So here's my plan. It may not be the best, and if you know a better one, that's okay. The main thing is to have one.

To put the giant back to sleep, I think you have to start over in your relationship. Don't make any sexual noise at all, and even when you're sure the giant is asleep, talk in whispers.

For a start, give up going out alone. Talk on the phone and see each other in groups or with another couple, but don't stay alone and don't touch. It'll be hard. It'll wrench your relationship out of the intimacy you've known into a louder, busier world you've half forgotten. In the process, you may get to know each other much better, and see each other with clearer eyes. But it won't be easy or comfortable. That's the penalty you pay for waking the giant.

Then, when you are *sure* things are under control — which is about the time, I'd say, when a date alone isn't all that different or more exciting than going out with a group — you can go out again. But make sure you set some careful guidelines for yourselves, and help each other keep them. Don't wake up the giant (he's a light sleeper) or you'll have to start over again.

A Love Story

All this will seem crazy. It will frustrate you less if you laugh at it and treat it as a game. Laughter is a sign of health in a serious relationship. Best wishes.

Today is my half-birthday. Today, I am exactly eighteen years and six months old. I've considered myself a Christian for about the past two-and-a-half years, but one thing keeps causing me to fall.

I used to be a real freak. Pills, rebellion, sex, the whole bit. Well, I've kicked the pills, and I have a beautiful peace within me, but I just don't have the will power to say no to sex. I know it's wrong, but I'd only be lying to myself if I denied enjoying it.

The last time was just last week. Sam, a guy I met by going out with his best friend, was moving away. He came over to say good-by. We went out, and suddenly he just kissed me. He said he was all confused, because he's always liked me, and now he was moving across the country. Well, we went to his apartment, and one thing led to another. I'm sure I don't have to spell it out. But—I loved it! I just felt so wonderful when he held me. I can't say I didn't want more and more and more. For that reason, it's hard for me to feel guilty about it at all.

I want to please God. Marriage and a family are so important to me. I just have this big problem I can't handle alone any more.

DON'T THINK YOU'RE abnormal. Not everyone has your specific problem, but just about everyone stumbles over what you're discovered: there's pleasure in doing wrong. Sometimes guilt can overwhelm the pleasure, but most of the time the pleasure comes through strongly.

How does God look at this? On the one hand, He's unhappy about your failures, and wants you to overcome. He wishes you were thinking of Him more and leaning on Him harder at those specific moments of temptation.

On the other hand, He's pleased that you've made progress. He doesn't pick you up one day, throw you back down when you've failed, pick you up when you get "resaved," and throw you back down when there's another failure. He's holding you all the time. He knows you aren't perfect. But He's looking forward to seeing you grow closer to what He meant you to be.

Stay in touch with the growing you've done. You've quit drugs. You feel more in touch with yourself. Thank God! Even in sex, you're more in control than you were. Failing occasionally is much better than giving up. God can deal with failure, if you bring it to Him. He has a much harder time helping you if you quit.

First, obviously, you ought to avoid the wrong situations — such as going alone to the apartment of a guy who kisses you and says he's "all confused." That is, I hope you know, a very old line. The intelligent time to resist was then, not later.

More important, I think, is to think out how you feel about different guys. How committed is the relationship? When you really analyze it, how much love is there to express? If you've thought through your relationships, you'll have something to counteract the temptation with. Tell yourself, "Grow up! I'm not committed that way! Neither is he! The romantic feelings are just a lie I want to believe."

I go to a Christian high school. Recently some popular kids have come to the conclusion that there should be No physical contact whatsoever before marriage – no holding hands, kissing, etc. One verse they use is 1 Corinthians 7:1, which says it's good for a man not to touch a woman. What do you think?

I THINK IT'S a perfectly valid decision for someone to make about himself — but not to foist on someone else. The Bible's support for their position is weak, since making out simply wasn't an issue in those times. The verse they're quoting is usually understood by experts, because of its context, to mean, "The single life is a good option." If they prefer to read it more literally, outside the context of the chapter, then they ought to take it literally all the way and say

Paul is suggesting that marriage, too, is a bad option since it requires a man to "touch."

While I think it's okay for someone to make a personal "hands off" decision, I do wonder about the motives behind it. In other contexts I've seen entire groups of Christians opt in favor of only having "brother-sister" relationships. I'm all for quality nonromantic friendships between the sexes; I wish we had more. But I think most of the time these mass-group decisions are based on fear. The guys are copping out because they're basically still afraid of girls, and are incapable of forming good friendships with them. Both sexes are afraid of their sexuality — afraid of getting carried away, and disliking the strong emotions that sexuality brings up.

But in my Bible it says God created us in His image, "male and female." There's something of God's nature in our sexuality! And that element of God's personality doesn't appear the day I marry. I'm a male today.

Naturally, there are risks involved in any touching. (There are risks in being human, too.) You could get carried away. You could get rejected. Sex could dominate your relationships. But I think God wants us to risk. For most people, romantic relationships, including some "touching," are part of learning about themselves and the opposite sex.

When a good-looking girl walks by at school, it's almost like a joke. Someone says, "Boy, would I like to get her in bed," or something like that. I've never really thought that much about these remarks; everyone makes them.

Then I read in the Bible where Jesus says, "Anyone who looks at a woman with lust in his eye has already committed adultery with her in his heart." So are those comments as bad as actually having sex with the girl? What is lust, anyway? Sometimes I think about sex. Is that wrong?

THE TRUTH IS, there isn't an agreed-on answer to "what is lust?" Wonderful, thoughtful Christians disagree on a definition, and the Bible doesn't give one. The Greek word translated "lust" literally means a neutral "strong desire" — its positive or negative meaning is to be taken from the context.

Obviously the main point Jesus is making is that it's not just the actions you make that God is concerned with. God looks at what's going on inside your head, too. We're all in need of forgiveness where sex is concerned, because whether we restrain ourselves or not, our attitudes often are wrong. No one else knows about them, but God does.

What is the "wrong attitude"? There are two schools of thought, generally. One sees the problem in your thought life. If you're fantasizing various sexual exploits with a girl, playing an X-rated movie in your head and letting the girl turn into a sex object, that's lust. The lust doesn't come from the initial thought — that's the temptation — but from giving in and letting it take over a nice, moist corner of your mind. Some imagination of sex is natural, but you shouldn't let it go on at length.

The other school thinks the problem is in the will. If the only thing holding you back from having sex with the girl is fear of being caught, or a rejection, then you're as guilty as the guy who goes out and does it.

I don't know, and the Bible doesn't make clear which of these is the right way to understand what Jesus said. There are many variations on these definitions, too. But I think we can say that any time we let sex dehumanize another person, so that he or she isn't a person but an object, it's wrong. And if the only difference between you and the guy who has sex is that you're afraid, you're also in need of mental repair. You are responsible to God for the way you think about another person. No one knows what you think. There isn't a good rule book on what's proper and what isn't. But I think you can make some intelligent observations about what's destructive in your life.

As for the comments, I'm not sure they necessarily represent lust. They are rude, dehumanizing, and thoughtless. But for many guys they're less lust than a crude way of saying "she looks good." Whichever is the case with you, you could live without them.

A Love Story

3

Masturbation

Very often what God first helps us toward is not the virtue itself but just this power of always trying again.

C. S. Lewis, Mere Christianity

I have a problem. *I don't want to disappoint the Lord or sin against Him. I have been a Christian for two years. My question is this: is it wrong to masturbate? I read my Bible a lot and haven't found anything specific. My parents think it's normal but they aren't Christians. I can't ask anyone else for fear of their thinking I'm "abnormal." Please tell me what you think.*

THIS LETTER REPRESENTS one of the most common, most emotional questions I hear. What I think depends on what day you ask me. Some days I am sure masturbation is wrong, and others I am sure it is okay. On the whole, I have to answer with three unpopular words: *I don't know.* I wish I had a better answer, because I know how this problem can tear a person apart.

But some good can come from simply talking about it honestly. Besides, I think I know every possible argument on either side. So I'd like to summarize those arguments, throwing in some comments along the way. Perhaps you'll be helped, and reach a conclusion of your own.

Let me begin with the arguments that masturbation is okay.

The silence of God. The strongest argument in favor of masturbation is simply that the Bible does not say a single word about it. If someone says he's found a passage that deals directly with it, he's misunderstood the passage. A few passages offer general principles which could be used against maturbation, but scholars disagree about their application. In any case, why couldn't God be explicit if He wanted to be? Just about every other aspect of sinful sexuality is covered, from homosexuality to adultery — but not a word is said about masturbation. Could that be because it wasn't a problem then? That's inconceivable to me; human sexuality simply can't have changed that much. The Bible is silent, and those who think masturbation is okay say that's because it's morally neutral, and a fairly trivial aspect of growing up. The burden of proof is on those who claim it's wrong.

Physiological necessity. Herbert J. Miles, in *Sexual Understanding Before Marriage*, points out that males have a regular buildup of semen which must be expelled somehow. That's simply a medical fact. There are three ways it can be expelled: in sexual intercourse, in masturbation, or through nocturnal emissions (wet dreams). Miles claims that for some, at certain stages, wet dreams simply won't take the pressure off adequately. It's either sex or masturbation, and for a single Christian, masturbation is the only choice. If God designed our bodies so that masturbation is at times the only alternative to having sex, wouldn't that indicate that masturbation strictly for the purpose of self-control (but not necessarily for pleasure) is okay? Miles thinks so, and suggests doing it with an attitude of thanks to God. But he suggests that girls, because there is no *physiological* pressure toward sex for them, shouldn't masturbate at all.

Others suggest that the psychological pressures are just as compelling, and apply to girls just as much as to guys.

Escape valve. Miles sees masturbation in very cautious terms: it's useful only under certain narrow circumstances. The escape valve argument takes this farther, and sees it as a positive good — a "gift from God." In this view, masturbation is an escape valve for the sex drive. If you couldn't masturbate, you'd be likely to get carried away with your girl friend or boyfriend.

I think this is a weak argument. Statistics don't support it. The Sorenson Report found that those who've had sex tend to masturbate more than those who haven't, not less. It's true that guys who've had sex within the last month tend to masturbate in that period slightly less often, but girls who've had sex that month masturbate substantially more! Masturbation and sex are not an either/or proposition. If you're counting on masturbation to lower your appetite for the opposite sex, you're likely to be disappointed.

Personally, I think the safety-valve argument has the wrong idea about sex, anyway: it compares sex to live steam which has to either escape or explode. (Incidentally, that's why some say masturbation will be easier to fight if you wear yourself out playing sports. My own informal findings are that while sports may help take your mind off sex, there's no transfer of sexual energy. If there were, wouldn't football players and hard-working construction crews be the least sexual of all?)

A Love Story

Most of us aren't, I think, drawn to sex because of strictly physical pressures. It's a mental and emotional attraction. At this level, I think sex works just the opposite of steam under pressure. If you keep putting sex in its place, it becomes easier to control. However, if you "let off pressure" through having intercourse, looking at pornography or masturbating, sex seems to wake up and demand more activity!

In marriage that's a good thing, not a bad thing. And it offers some hope to single people too — that the more you control your sexual drives, the easier they become to control.

To be fair to those who propose this escape-valve theory, I think many of them are trying to counteract the morbid guilt many feel about masturbating, and in doing so overstate their case. The arguments for masturbation make a strong case together. The Bible says nothing. Some experts believe that for some, some of the time, masturbation is a physiological necessity. And everyone agrees that no physical harm can come as a result of it. So what possible basis can there be for moralizing against it? Naturally masturbation isn't the wonderful thing sex in marriage is — but isn't it better to live peaceably with it than to be obsessed by guilt? Those on this side suggest, usually, that those who consider masturbation sinful are simply carrying over the antisex bias of the past, with no real biblical or rational basis for their beliefs.

And now, the arguments against masturbation.

Guilt. David Wilkerson sums it up well: "Efforts to remove guilt and fear by the experts have miserably failed. Told that masturbation is normal, fun, legitimate and even a gift of God, teenagers still say, 'Then why do I still feel so guilty about it?'" In other words, our consciences are more reliable than the pronouncements of experts, and our consciences proclaim 'Guilty!'"

But I have to add some qualifiers to this argument. In the first place, not everyone feels guilty. The Sorenson Report reported that over half of all adolescents who masturbate say they rarely or never feel guilty about it. Could it be those who feel guilty project their own feelings on others?

Also, the conscience is *not* an infallible guide. We know that Eichmann, who slaughtered thousands of Jews, claimed to believe he had done nothing wrong, and felt not a twinge of remorse. The opposite happens, too: you can feel guilty about something that isn't wrong. Some married women, they tell me, feel guilty about enjoying sex because they've been taught sex is dirty.

Still, I have to rate guilt as a powerful argument. The amount of guilt some feel is astonishing: many, many kids express in the bitterest language possible how filthy and repulsive they feel as a result of masturbation. These aren't twinges of guilt: they are deep-seated expressions of self-hatred. There are various explanations of this — some say, for instance, that since masturbation is an introspective, solitary affair, it's natural for all kinds of guilt to attach to it. Most teenagers feel guilty and worthless about many aspects of their life; in *Sex for Christians* Lewis Smedes suggests that they attach a lot of that self-hate to the naturally unfulfilling act of masturbation.

But I'm left with a nagging question of whether that much guilt can be explained. Is it a genuine guilt before God, as Wilkerson suggests?

Fantasy. A common argument against masturbation is that it often is associated with lurid fantasies. "If you could do it without lusting in your fantasy life, there'd be nothing wrong," this argument goes. "But you can't. When you're imagining sexual gymnastics with the opposite sex, living it up in your head, you're doing just what Jesus condemned in Matthew 5:28: everyone who looks on a woman to lust for her has committed adultery with her already in his heart."

At one time I thought this was an invulnerable argument. Now I know it isn't. It offers a particular interpretation and extension of what Jesus said, one that many conservative Bible scholars simply don't buy. The fantasy argument identifies "lust" with "fantasize." But the Greek word translated "lust" doesn't imply that. According to *The New Bible Dictionary*, the word *epithymia* "expresses any strong desire, the context or a qualifying adjective determining its nature. . . ." It's the same word Paul uses when he says a friend of his "longs" for his friends he left behind. Jesus used it when He said to His disciples, "I have *earnestly desired* to eat this Passover with you" (Luke 22:15). Many Bible scholars would suggest that Jesus' statement in Matthew 5:28 means something like this: "When you deliberately look at a woman (or a man) strictly as a sex object, dehumanizing her (or him), then you're as guilty of sexual infidelity as someone who actually goes ahead and acts out the plan." That has some similarities to fantasy — it's all in your head. But it isn't the same as the sexual imaginings most people have while masturbating (and many have when making love). Some imagining about sex is natural. I doubt anyone has to look up details in a sex manual on his wedding night. Is that bad?

Furthermore, it's normal to dream about sex — especially for guys during "wet dreams." Is that bad?

And not everyone fantasizes when he or she masturbates: about 10% of all adolescents say they never do. Are 10% right in masturbating while the other 90% are wrong? I have a friend who can't understand what people mean when they talk about "fantasizing" sex — he simply can't make his mind do that. Does that make him moral while I stay immoral?

One reason the fantasy argument is advanced is that people say there's a "thought cycle" involved: that the way you think determines the way you act. At one level this is undoubtedly true: a person who thinks selfishly usually acts selfishly. But it may not be true of fantasizing specific acts. At least the statistics don't find it for this: those who fantasize when they masturbate have premarital sex about as often as those who don't fantasize when they masturbate.

Still, some kind of Christian mind control is called for. We're not to let our minds roam free. We're to think good thoughts. And masturbation does raise the questions: are these fantasies the kind of thoughts that build me up? Are they healthy? Are they thankful and in tune with God? And is there any way to clean up my thoughts while continuing to masturbate?

Crutch. Many point out that masturbation, like drugs, can be a way of withdrawing from the world and never facing your problems. It can become compulsive and obsessive. It's a crutch, a poor way of dealing with feelings of loneliness.

No doubt this often is true. But when you consider that 70-90% of the guys and 50-70% of the girls masturbate, you're in the position of suggesting there are an awful lot of cripples. It makes more sense to me to say that masturbation *can* be a crutch.

Homosexuality. There are those who say that masturbation is a form of homosexuality, leading to overt homosexuality of the worst kind. This argument strikes me as nonsense. There is no known statistical correlation between the two. No doubt many homosexuals masturbate, but they also drink milk, I'd bet.

Second rate. Many argue that masturbation is wrong primarily because it is second-rate sex. Sex was made for intense communication between two people knit together in a permanent relationship — a relationship that is an example, on a small scale, of what our relationship to God is becoming. It is fitting, too, that all of us begin our lives through sex's collaboration of love and joy: it says something that God wants us created in this way rather than in some possibly more efficient way. (We could germinate, boringly, like geraniums.)

Masturbation loses all those benefits of sex. It produces nothing except fleeting pleasure: no love for another, no children. Sex is meant to be shared, and masturbation, because it is selfish, is directly opposed to what sex is for.

This is an unanswerably powerful argument. The very best we can say of masturbation is that it is second-best — a kind of delaying action until something better comes along. That certainly fits the data — I don't know of anyone *proud* of masturbating.

Many would go further with this argument. Because masturbation is selfish, they'd say, it takes us away from a healthy way of looking at sex. It destroys one of the most precious things we have: our ideal of the beautiful sharing of sexuality.

Not from faith. Paul wrote, "Anything that is not of faith is sin." Some say that, just because we can't decide conclusively whether masturbation is right or not, we ought to stay away from it. One man said that, since he wasn't sure whether he could safely stay on the road if he drove over on the edge of the cliff, he'd prefer to stay on the safe side where he knew he was okay. Unless you're absolutely *sure* masturbation is right, you shouldn't do it.

A Love Story

But the argument can be turned around. You're not sure masturbation is wrong, either. So should you expend all the energy and sweat most people put out trying to stop? Isn't that, too, an action fueled by doubt?

After reading these arguments, you probably think I'm really for one or the other position, and am playing cute by saying I'm undecided. I've been accused of that by people on both sides of the fence. However, I'm not shy about expressing my beliefs. I just don't know. I've tried to give the arguments as accurately as possible. If you think these arguments promote one point of view, that may be because the facts really run that way, at least for you. As for me, I'm unsure.

Whatever your conclusion, I doubt these basic facts will change: people will still masturbate, and many will still feel frustrated and guilty because they aren't able to stop. I could write myself blue about whether it's wrong or right. I'd rather offer some help for those caught in the middle. Let me try.

First of all, I think you ought to realize masturbation is about as normal — normal in the sense of "average" — as you can get. That doesn't make it right — but it might relieve some of the tension you feel. I think you ought to know that most people who "preach" to you about it — including me — have struggled with it. It's likely most of your friends masturbate, as do many of the adults you know. (Incidentally, marriage is not necessarily a remedy for masturbation; neither is growing older, though many people do quit as their sex drive lessens with age.) I suspect some of those who rail most bitterly against the evils of masturbation feel most guilty themselves.

One thing I'm sure of: masturbation is no big deal. If it's a sin, it's one the Bible deals with less than gossip, overeating, and kicking the cat. Why can't we take up God's priorities? Why should we expend all our energy worrying about this, when there are other things in our lives He is more deeply concerned about?

If you feel deeply guilty about masturbation, you need some help defusing those powerful emotions of self-hatred.

That is *not* the way God looks at you; you ought to stop beating yourself into the ground. One help is to talk to some strong, sympathetic Christian about your problem. I know, from experience, that sharing your struggles can be agonizing. But it also can be very liberating. You need to experience acceptance from other people; you need to let out the inner pressure. Self-acceptance comes through others' acceptance of you. Accepting yourself could help you deal with masturbation more than anything else — at least by letting you put your mind on more important things.

"But I want to quit," some say. "Whether it's wrong for everyone or not, I believe it's wrong for me. I don't want to accept it. I want to *quit* it."

Frankly, you may not be able to. Some are, and many of them are very happy about it. But most people suffer through years of trying to quit. They try all kinds of remedies, and nothing works. I wish I didn't have to be discouraging, but I think some realism is called for. If you want to quit, I encourage that, of course. But I hope you'll be prepared to accept and love yourself as God does if you fail.

How to quit? I have heard all kinds of antidotes, from playing a lot of football to praying many prayers; from giving yourself pep talks to going to bed late and getting up early. All of these must have worked at least once for at least one person. My own experience, however, as well as the experience of many others who've shared with me, indicates that none of them works terribly well.

The only remedy I'd wholeheartedly recommend is taking your eyes off yourself and turning them outward. Masturbation, and the guilt arising from it, can turn you inward toward a lonely fantasy world instead of the world of people. It's a negative cycle: the guilt turns you inward, and the inwardness leads to more loneliness, which leads to more masturbation. The way out, I believe, is for God to take those thoughts and temptations on Himself, and leave you free. Ask Him to do that, and let Him. He certainly is capable of it.

Going to God in complete desperation may be your only choice at times, but the best way to reach Him is with a grateful heart, a peaceful heart, a trusting heart. Desperation turns you inward; you may try to talk to God, but I think you often end up talking to your own fears. Be grateful for what God has done. Gratefulness helps take your mind off yourself, and puts it on God.

You also ought to look to people. Jay Kesler, president of YFC, has pointed out that what we think is a sex problem often is really a life problem. Masturbation, for instance, may be the expression of loneliness. Solving the loneliness by taking concrete steps to make friends may solve the masturbation problem. Even if you keep masturbating, it will be less compulsive.

More important than whether or not you quit masturbation is, I think, keeping a clear view of the beauty of sex. One of the worst effects of masturbation is that it has made millions loathe their bodies and their sexuality. That's tragic.

One way of staying positive in your outlook is to eliminate perverted ways of thinking. You may not be able to stop fantasizing about sex, but you can limit your fantasies to positive subjects. Nothing good will come from fantasies about group sex, homosexuality, and rape. I doubt that using pornography is ever a good idea, if only because it presents such a depersonalized vision of sex. I think imagining sex with someone you know as a friend is a mistake — a misuse of that person that could carry over into your relationship.

But it's not enough to stay away from these things: you need to have some positive input. Have you thought hard about the practical beauties of marriage? Can you appreciate the lovely role sexuality plays between all men and women, the way it weaves our lives in and out of each other's? Can you take delight in the tingle it adds to all your relationships? Can you appreciate particularly the potential it has to seal two people together as one body — a union of two personalities, two minds, two spirits, two bodies? Have you thought of that as an analogy to our relationship with Christ? If masturbation should distract us from appreciating these things, it is indeed a great evil.

* * * *

The letter that began this chapter, and most of the comments you've read so far, were printed in *Campus Life* magazine. As you can imagine, there were many letters in response — both positive and negative. Two who wrote made particularly good points in attacking masturbation.

▶ **God is silent on masturbation.** He is also silent on drug addiction, but the general declaration that we are the temples of God guides us. Don't we have some guidelines on questionable things like masturbation? Like — "But fornication, and all uncleanness . . . let it not be once named among you. . . . For it is a shame even to speak of those things which are done of them in secret" (Eph. 5:3a,12).

Timothy was a young man and his spiritual advisor stressed "a pure heart," "good conscience," "pure conscience," "an example to the believers in purity." "Be strong," he said, "endure hardness," "flee also youthful lusts." "For men shall be lovers of pleasures more than lovers of God, having a form of godliness, but denying the power thereof; from such turn away."

Isn't the real problem that we want to listen to suggestive music, watch suggestive TV and movies, read suggestive magazines, spend time petting with our current heartthrob and then blame God for our "biological" urges?

There is one quote I wish you would put in caps. John Wesley's mother once wrote him:

"Whatsoever weakens your reason, impairs the tenderness of your conscience, obscures your sense of God, or takes off the relish of spiritual things — whatsoever increases the authority of your body over your mind — that thing, to you, is sin."

▶ **1. As I read my Bible it says to me** that sex was created to be used in the marriage union only, between husband and wife. If so, then having sexual pleasures by yourself is just as sinful as committing adultery.

2. If you take percentages as making something normal or right, does that make premarital sex right because such a high percentage of people are having it? No! The fact that a high percentage of people masturbate doesn't make it right or normal.

3. The Bible says you should have "self-control." Any habit you can't control is sinful. When you have lost your self-control then who *is* in control?

4. If so many Christians are feeling guilty about masturbating, then maybe the Holy Spirit is trying to tell them something. I

A Love Story

think a Christian can trust his conscience more than a non-Christian.

5. Don't limit the power of Jesus. If Jesus can help young people get off drugs, help people quit smoking, or help an alcoholic quit drinking, why couldn't He help a person stop masturbating?

Many of the points mentioned in these letters I wholeheartedly agree with. A few need to be commented on.

1. The first letter assumes that "lust" and "uncleanness" include masturbation. Emotionally I find it easy to make that leap, but my mind tells me the association could be wrong: I might feel that masturbation is filthy just because my background has taught me that. The silence of the Bible on drug addiction isn't a good parallel, because drugs (with the exception of alcohol, whose overuse is condemned) weren't commonly available when the Bible was written. And anyway, we all believe drugs should be used, carefully and responsibly, when a doctor prescribes them.

2. A big question is whether, as the second letter says, "sex was created to be used in the marriage union only." Many Christians assume that any influence of sex in their lives before marriage is, if not lust, at least an influence that diverts their attention from God. I disagree, respectfully. Sex is part of our lives, as God made us. The question is, "What's a *good* way to express our sexual feelings?"

3. Self-control is a tricky question. The Bible urges us to have it, but you can get carried away with the idea. If you take John Wesley's mother literally, I think you have gone too far. If this is an argument against masturbation, then it is also an argument against sleep or falling in love. In those cases, too, you can't stop doing it, it obscures your sense of God, and it increases the control of your body and your emotions over your will.

The debate over masturbation is still going on, and I think both sides have a lot to say. I wish I could settle the issue with one slash of the pen, but I can't. You'll have to decide for yourselves. You *should* remember, always, that masturbation is not No. 1 on God's list of priorities. If it were, He would have said so.

Christian Answers on Sex

That's why one letter in particular, of all I've seen on masturbation, means the most to me. It was sent to the editor of *Campus Life*, and this is how it went:

▶ ⌐ I have read all of the comments on masturbation. All I want to say is that I appreciate the article and the honesty in printing it. You see, I'm the guy who wrote the original letter. The article helped me tremendously. Now I don't feel like such a pervert.

4

Singleness

A single person *is* the image of God; but he is God's image only when he personally relates in love to others.

Lewis Smedes, *Sex for Christians*

A lot of your letters seem to come from people worrying about whether they should have sex or not. That's not my problem. I worry whether I'll ever have a date.

I guess I've always assumed that sooner or later I'd get married. Now I am beginning to wonder. I'm not panicking, but when I see other girls with their boyfriends, I can't help but get depressed. That only makes things worse, of course. I don't really know what I'm asking, because no one can help me.

YOU'RE NOT ALONE. I've heard that 50% of the girls graduating from high school have never had a date. I don't know whether that figure is right or not, but I'm sure the majority of young people aren't, at any given time, dating anyone. They feel abnormal. but they really aren't. It's very likely they'll end up married — the vast majority of Americans do.

But no one can guarantee that. And I'd like to point out that no one should, because being single is the best way to live for a great many people.

That isn't the message coming through our society (or our churches). Our world has put sex on a very high pedestal, and along with it marriage or living-together relationships. To never make love, to never share the deepest personal intimacies with another person seems synonymous with being undesirable and possibly even perverted. I think it's largely this image which has made so many single people so unhappy. Being single isn't so bad in itself, but if negative attitudes dominate your mind, you'll be miserable.

Yet God may want you to be single. He wants everyone to be single for at least a part of life. And the Bible doesn't talk about singleness as second-rate. In fact, it speaks of it positively. In the Middle Ages Christians went too far, and *marriage* was regarded as second-rate. We seem to have swung the other way now, and need to balance in the middle. Both marriage and singleness are gifts from God.

Ponder for a minute one fact: Jesus Christ, our Lord, never married. He never had sexual intercourse. Yet He was perfect, and perfectly fulfilled. He lived the kind of life we want to imitate. That doesn't mean we ought to all want to be single: there's no doubt marriage is the best way for most men and women. But it should say one thing for certain: singleness need not be second-rate. It need not be unfulfilled. It need not be unhappy. When well-meaning people ask me, "What's a nice guy like you doing without a wife?" I sometimes answer, with a grin, "I'm just hoping to be more like Jesus!"

Paul wasn't married either, at least at the height of his career. He wrote recommending the single life in 1 Corinthians 7, calling it a gift. (Strange that this is the one gift most would prefer to exchange.) And Jesus Himself, in Matthew 19:10-12, talks positively about the reasons some people should remain unmarried.

Some people, of course, try to peer into the future and find out whether God has given them the gift of singleness. They want to know, I guess, whether someday God is going to award them a spouse, or whether they should forget about relating to the opposite sex, shrug their shoulders, and settle down to the long grind. Maybe God does actually tell some people ahead of time whether they will or won't be married. But most of us seem to find out what He wants one day at a time. I have no reason to believe that a "gift" of singleness can't be temporary. God may completely fulfill you as a single person at one stage of life, but at another He might call you to marriage. By the same token, a married man, for example, never knows when his spouse's death might call him back to the "gift" of singleness.

One of the saddest things I see, then, is the tendency for single people to live life as though waiting for something or someone to happen to them. They act as though they are in limbo, waiting to become capable of life when the magic day at the altar comes. Of course, they're usually disappointed. In some cases they become such poor specimens of humanity that no one wants to marry them. More often they do get married only to discover that they haven't received the key to life: the initiative and character they should have developed before marriage is exactly what they need in marriage. And they are still lonely and frustrated.

What do you do with a gift? You open it. You admire it. You thank the giver. You use it. And this is what we ought to do with the singleness God has called us to for the present.

Much has been written about the special opportunities a single person has. There is, as Paul points out in 1 Corinthians 7:32-34, greater freedom for someone without a family to care for — freedom to help other people, freedom to spend time with God, freedom to develop himself, freedom to have fun. But this gift, however good, is worth little unless it is put to use. Our culture, especially our Christian culture, has stressed repeatedly that a good marriage takes work. It holds up for admiration those who have formed "a good marriage." But I've seldom heard anyone emphasize the fact that a good single life also takes work. I've never heard anyone compliment a person for having created a good single life style. This creates an atmosphere in which telling single people they have received a gift is rather like convincing a small child that liver ought to taste good, because it's "good for you."

Singleness, as I see it, is not so much a state we've arrived at as an open door, a set of opportunities for us to follow up.

Let me name some specifics. There are certain things most people need, single or married, and one is what Walter Trobisch calls a "place." It's simply appalling how often single people live in dumps, with no privacy and no attractiveness, nevertheless looking dreamily forward to the day when they can establish a "home of their own." Home means different things to different people. It may imply a well-stocked kitchen where good meals are prepared regularly. It may imply having guests over. It may mean flowers on the table, or a nice bedspread on the bed, or a chance for some privacy. It may mean relationships in which you're really comfortable. Not one of those things is impossible for single people. In fact, single people usually have more time and money to invest in them. And they do make a major difference in the quality of life. I know that when I come in the door I need to find home. I don't need to find a messy environment that has the look and feel of a run-down motel. I need a sense of permanency. I need the kind of place where I'm delighted to have friends over for dinner. Establishing that kind of place is more, not less, crucial for single people than for married people. It takes time. It takes money. And it may require, if you live with roommates, talking out ahead of time the kind of place you want to make, and then making some commitments.

Let me be specific again. Most single people, at least while they're young, live with roommates. It can be pleasant and it can be horrible. Some of the horrors come, not from conflicting personalities, but from an unwillingness to be committed to each other.

If what you want is a place to sleep, you don't need commitment. So long as you can coexist, you're all right. But community only begins, normally, when you talk out specifically your commitment to each other and the place you're living in. Meals together are, I think, a crucial aspect of community, but you usually have to demand commitment to a minimum number of nights a week. Even if it's only one night a week, it ought to be a firm commitment that can't be broken because some friend invited you bowling. Some roommates establish a "family night" which they always reserve not only for a meal, but for a whole evening of sharing and praying together, or for just having fun. Some try to reserve a night when they invite friends over. It all takes commitment — including, of course, commitments to buy food together, to cook, to clean up, and to work out differences in taste. It's amazing how many squabbles come because someone leaves the bulk of the work to someone else. Sometimes you need to put those commitments down in writing ahead of time.

Other commitments are called for. For instance: how long do you plan to live there? Will you make a commitment for a full year, so that you're not leaving partners in the lurch? How about commitment to a certain, defined level of neatness? And how about a radical commitment to try to discuss things that are annoying you? If you don't (and it's always easier not to) your sense of community will fade away.

So much for "place." Another neglected aspect of singleness is developing yourself — doing something with your life. Of course, many single people pour themselves into their work. That's fine, so long as it's something you want to do and feel is important. For most of us, though, work isn't enough to live on. We need more variety. One woman, writing about her single years, was thankful she'd used those years to learn to play the piano. Others commit themselves to working in church, to doing volunteer work, to helping married friends with their children, to throwing good parties for a growing circle of friends of both sexes. (One great gift is good friends of your own sex. Our quest for a marriage partner often makes us neglect them.) There is opportunity to get to know God better, unhassled with family responsibilities. There are classes to take, poems to write, political candidates to work for. There simply isn't any need to sit at home lonely, waiting for Prince or Princess Charming. Being single gives you time to develop yourself, and to participate in things that are really worthwhile and interesting. Married people often look back on the opportunities they had while single and groan.

One other thing about being single: it doesn't mean you are sexless. Some single people think they are. They show it by the way they dress and the way they act. Even more often, they show it in their dull relationships.

But God has made us sexual creatures, and to try and deny that is to deny part of ourselves. Two kinds of relationships teach us about our sexuality the most: friendships between the sexes, and friendships with married people.

It's hard, when you're single, to have a solid friendship with someone of the opposite sex, because you and everyone around you are looking to see romance developing. That pressure makes a good friendship hard to form. I don't know any magic for overcoming the barriers, but I do know that it's possible. It gets easier, too, after the first few times. Initiating friendship is not up to guys alone, I should point out: any girl who doesn't know how to throw a party or invite a guy over for dinner should be trained. These friendships help you remember what it's like to be a sexual person: that is, a man or a woman. They also keep you from making the opposite sex into a mysterious, magical symbol. They remind you that all humans have much in common: they laugh, they smell, they feel lonely at times.

It helps to break out of the dating cycle, which normally builds up romantic expectations. It takes creativity, but it is possible to do other things together than go to a movie or eat dinner. How about doing some jogging together? Building a bookcase? Cooking some extraordinary dessert? Taking in a baseball game? And of course, getting a good group of people together dodges the romantic pressures. It's not that romance is a bad idea. Quite the opposite. But sometimes people get forgotten in the ceaseless quest for a partner.

Most single people are tempted to check out each new acquaintance, wondering whether he or she is the one for them. But there may not be "one for you." There certainly isn't more than one — most of your relationships will end unromantically, because God calls you to marry a maximum of one.

But He has called us to love everyone we meet, whether they are initially attractive or not, and even after a romantic relationship has failed to work out. Too often a breakup ends all contact. Too often attractive couples form but leave out everyone else. It's far healthier, far more Christian, when a commitment to care for each other begins and continues regardless of whether things "work out."

Even harder than forming good relationships between the sexes is forming good relationships with married couples. But this is important, too. There is a dividing wall between couples and singles, and it's difficult to break down. Couples will tend to invite you over only when they are hoping to match you with someone. You'll tend not to invite couples over to your house at all, because, for an undefined reason, singles don't entertain couples. But break the barriers. Actually, couples often are as isolated as single people. They need the friendship too.

Their value goes beyond simple friendship. You can learn something from them. In the first place, you can learn something realistic about marriage. You can learn that no two couples relate in the same way. You can learn that married people suffer some of the same troubles you do: they get lonely, and bored, and feel sorry for themselves. You can learn that marriage isn't synonymous with heaven.

And you can learn something about God. Marriage, you know, is the image God uses to describe His own relationship with us. The "likeness of God" is found especially in the intimacy of marriage; the submissive, all-giving love we're to have toward God is found there too. And children are important: how many lessons of the Bible are expressed in the relationship of children to their parents? It's not enough to read about these things: we need to be involved in them.

Families are the human drama. They are the soap opera that runs nonstop, and that everyone follows. They are the morality play God has written key lessons into.

The way some Christians see this, everyone ought to be married. Otherwise, they can't be "whole," since only in marriage do we find our complementary half.

But that isn't the Bible's way of looking at it. Marriage is a metaphor, a play, between two whole people. Each person is complete in himself, but two come together to make a drama impossible for just one. It takes a full cast of characters to play *Hamlet*. One actor can't play all the roles himself.

But when we talk about drama, we have to mention the audience, too. If you've ever been in a play you know that acting gives you a unique insight into the play. You don't understand a character fully until you've entered his life and played his part.

But sitting in the audience you have a completely different, and equally important, view of the play. The actor knows all the inside stuff: why one actor dropped his line, and the hilarious history of one of the goofs someone made. But he doesn't really know, for sure, whether the play is any good. From the audience you understand the play another way: more objectively. You can compare it with other versions of the same play. You can compare it with other plays. Your insights are just as valuable as the actors'.

That is how it is with us single people. We are the audience to the marriage drama. We need to learn from it. It is a fascinating drama to watch, full of meaning for our lives.

I encourage you to make friends with married couples.

If you've been single long, I guess this theorizing probably sounds idealistic. You know the dissatisfaction and the loneliness. You know the pain.

But what you don't know is the pain of being married. It's a different kind of pain. Some — especially those who struggle to keep their marriage alive, or who've already seen it shattered by divorce or death — would say the pain is much greater. Marriage has its own problems. Every way of life does — problems you don't discover or understand until you're experiencing them. God uses pain in every way of life to bring us closer to Him.

The trouble is, we mistake the message. We blame our loneliness on our circumstances. Thus, single people tend to blame all their problems on not being married, or on the fact that they don't have a close boyfriend or girl friend. Married people, or people going steady, tend to blame the feelings on their relationship. It's always greener on the other side of the fence.

Instead, we ought to accept loneliness, and use it as a basis for growing closer to God, ourselves, and others. It's helpful to me to remember that we're all ending up in the same place. Jesus reported there are no marriages in heaven. However different the experience of married and single people is here on earth, God is trying to develop the same kinds of qualities in us — qualities that make us ready to live with Him. Along the path He gives us — the "gift" of singleness, or the "gift" of marriage — there is going to be pain and frustration and loneliness. But there is also, for those willing to find it, joy with the knowledge that God loves you and is offering the best life He can give.

5

Homosexuality

Man . . . is the only animal capable of chastity.

Dwight Small, *Christian, Celebrate Your Sexuality*

My problem is different from most, and I don't know what to do. I am constantly being driven by homosexual desires. I don't even like to print that, but I guess I must say it. I know God loves me, but somehow I just can't seem to get things together. Why am I this way in the first place? People don't know how I hurt on the inside.

I've tried to help myself but I can't. I'm terribly lonely. I've thought about talking to my minister, but I can't. He thinks I'm a terrific guy. If he only knew what I am going through.

DUE TO RECEIVING many letters like this one, I feel queasy when I hear people joke about homosexuals. I wonder if someone is listening who is driven deeper into hating himself. You might be surprised — I know most people would be — at the number of people, Christian and non-Christian, male and female, who feel driven by homosexual desires and are confused and sick over it. Though it is not "normal," it is common.

If you are troubled by this kind of desire, I want to begin by repeating what you already know: that the Bible considers homosexual actions wrong. There isn't a great deal of material dealing with it; in the Old Testament it simply is declared off-limits, and that is carried over in the New Testament. The only passage that gives a hint of *why* it is wrong is Romans 1:26,27. There Paul discusses homosexuality in the context of a civilization that has turned its back on God, and has succeeded in twisting so far away from what it ought to be that it has exchanged what is "natural" for what is "unnatural." Paul probably is thinking of the story of creation in Genesis, where God made man in His own image "male and female." We're sexual people — that's what's "natural" — and sex was made to be between male and female. The trouble with homosexuality is that it doesn't let males be male and females be female, because male and female only mean something in relationship to each other. I don't mean that homosexuals are sick because some act effeminate — though the fact that some do might tell us something. I mean that they are closed off to their full human identity by not discovering themselves in relationship to the opposite sex.

We learn something about ourselves and about God through the wonderful erotic attraction and interaction of male and female. We learn even if we never marry, for we take part in those interactions at other levels.

That is the basic threat — that you would lose out on part of your identity. Your true identity in Christ isn't homosexual. Some experts say nearly everyone has homosexual desires to some extent. But the sexual focus of our lives ought to be the opposite sex, for that is how we discover more about ourselves.

There isn't any condemnation of homosexual tendencies in the Bible. Being attracted to your own sex is a temptation, a unique and difficult one. But temptation isn't sin; so long as you resist acting out your desires, or inflaming your mind by dwelling on them, you're not sinning. In fact, you may be growing closer to God by trusting Him for strength.

Nor does the Bible give any hint that homosexual sins are any worse than other kinds. If you look at the verses following Romans 1:26,27, you see that envy and gossip are in the same class.

So if you're sorry for past actions and have confessed them to God, and if you're ready to continue resisting temptation, with God's help, you're as good in God's eyes as anyone else.

But I know that assurance, while it helps, doesn't solve the problem. I imagine the central problem is expressed in the words, "I'm terribly lonely." That's a very common reaction. You can't talk to anyone because of the fear and the shame. You envy those who have normal dating relationships, but getting romantic with a girl just doesn't do much for you. You're afraid to get close to a guy, because you're not sure you could handle the temptations. Besides, if the guy found out, he might be totally repulsed. You end up closed off from the rest of the world, feeling miserable and lonely, full of self-pity. You wonder, "Why was I made this way?"

To that last question I don't think there's any final answer. One thing is clear: *It's not your fault.* Some researchers think it's an innate condition; others think it's psychological, the result of an overbearing mother or something like that. No one know what causes it, and no one knows why God has let it come to you. My own suspicion is that its cause has a lot to do with the kind of sexually confused society we live in. Walter Trobisch, a writer who lived in Africa for many years, says homosexuality is almost unknown there, except perhaps in port cities where there has been a Western influence. But if homosexuality is part of a willful condition in our society, that doesn't mean you're personally accountable. The condition has been given to you. You're accountable for how you respond.

Some homosexuals say that the right way to respond is "naturally." That is, "You have the condition; therefore, act it out. Be true to yourself." I think they're wrong, but why?

There are some obviously unhealthy aspects of homosexuality: the pick-up bars, the affected behavior, the short-lived relationships based on physical appearance. But there are also homosexuals who have tried to make the best of their condition by forming permanent "marriages" with someone of the same sex, giving love and affection just as they see married couples doing. Isn't that "natural" for them?

We may yet see compelling reasons why it is not "natural." But right now all I can say is that the Bible doesn't see it that way. The "natural" thing — the thing to do if you want to affirm who you really are, as God made you — is to resist homosexual temptations and try to affirm heterosex as much as it's possible for you. I don't expect non-Christians to accept this. But if we follow the Bible — and personally, I have found it to be far more reliable than my own logic — we have to follow it in saying that homosexual acts are unnatural.

Why are you tempted by them, while others aren't? Only God knows.

But it may help to realize that other people ask the same identical "Why? Why was I made this way?" Crippled people ask it; ugly people ask it; mute people ask it. In fact, nearly everyone asks it at one time or another. But it isn't a question that helps you. Self-pity only makes the situation worse.

I know a guy who has cerebral palsy. He can't talk at all, his hands are twisted so that he can't use them, and even his feet are unsteady so that he can barely walk. Yet his mind is completely intact, and he's completed college now, typing papers with his toes. He's got a good sense of humor (he scribbles out his conversations on the floor with his feet) and most people who try talking to him can't resist liking him.

I asked him once what was the most important way a person could help someone like him. He didn't have to stop and think: he immediately wrote out with his foot, "Don't pity us." He knew pity would cripple him sooner than his disease. And the guy doesn't pity *himself* at all. He could. He has every reason to. But he won't. He's accepted himself the way he is, and gone ahead with his life.

From what I can see, those with homosexual desires have the same basic problem. Self-pity destroys them as much as anything. You must resist this, and consistently ask God to help you resist it.

Then you can pray for God to change you. There are many homosexuals who've been "healed," some overnight, some over a long period of time. It doesn't happen to everyone, but it does happen to some. One guy wrote, "He has not only changed my sexual-physical desires, but also my ways of thinking, my actions and mannerisms, my interests and my self-image. His power is fantastic. It is also available to anyone. He has proven this in my life by giving me increasing heterosexual desires that have never before been present. God still changes lives today. I praise Him and thank Him. He has miraculously changed me!"

And there are others who tell the same story. I have to say that God doesn't change everyone. But do not give up on God. Be honest with Him day after day. Ask Him for help.

I'd recommend being honest with another person, too. This is very difficult because of the tragic attitudes many Christians have toward homosexuals. Pray this over carefully. The risks are great, but I think you should take them. Experiencing someone else's growing acceptance of you is part and parcel of growing to accept yourself. When you find someone you believe you can talk to, make sure you explain fully to him how afraid you are he'll reject you. Chances are he will initially be taken aback. But if he understands the need, and is really a mature Christian, he'll be willing to help you.

Finally, it's important to develop a life style you can

A Love Story

survive with. True, normal romance and marriage look pretty appealing. But it's made very clear in the Bible that some people are called by God to remain single, and that isn't considered a second-class life style. It hardly could be, since Jesus and Paul chose it.

The single life can be completely fulfilling. But like a good marriage, it takes work. You can't sit around waiting for a fulfilled life to be delivered in the mail. You have to deliberately cultivate the friendships (and often a group of friends is the best option) and interests that make life seem worth living. Every unmarried person faces this — you are no different from the rest of us.

Perhaps 1 Corinthians 10:13 will help you: "But remember this — the wrong desires that come into your life aren't anything new and different. Many others have faced exactly the same problems before you. And no temptation is irresistible. You can trust God to keep the temptation from becoming so strong that you can't stand up against it, for he has promised this and will do what he says. He will show you how to escape temptation's power so that you can bear up patiently against it" (LB).

6
Going Out

God invented sex, but dating is an American creation. Though the word "dating" has become somewhat passé, the practice is going strong. And a stranger custom cannot be found among primitive tribes anywhere.

Dating follows strict, unwritten rules which don't help people get to know each other at all; they heighten tension. Why must it always be the *guy's* car? (And why a car, always?) Why must girls who, in every other area of life seem capable of making decisions and expressing opinions, wait hopelessly for some nervous, shy guy to realize that she's staring at him in class because she wants to go out with him? Why does dating have to seal off even the most casual couple from the rest of the world, so that a mutual friend couldn't possibly join them without causing embarrassment? Dating seems like an antique, nostalgia on wheels.

There are some signs of reform — girls do sometimes ask guys out, for instance — and occasionally there is even an outspoken attack on the whole institution, as though the next wave of heightened consciousness would wash it away for good.

But I think dating will last a while. It will, hopefully, continue to become more flexible, but no one has come up with a better way for males and females to make their first shy encounters. Most of us simply are going to have to make the best of it we can.

I have gotten many letters on dating. Some of them are fairly amusing, such as the 11-year-old girl who wants to know if she's old enough to be going with someone; her girl friends tease her that she changes boys every month, but she's liked this one for *two* months. Much more common are the "I like Jimmy/Jane and sometimes we talk in class and he/she always smiles at me, do you think it's love?" letters. There are plenty of broken hearts, too, like this one: "A month ago he broke it off, saying he needs to be free. Then I found his freedom turned into another girl, who's 16. I still love him so much, and I just cry to be back again with him. . . ."

I'm happy to say most of these problems involve younger teenagers. I know how intense their problems feel, but I haven't any idea how to respond to them. So it relieves me to know that most people muddle through them. Anyone hoping to establish rules for other people's dating is on very shaky ground: no two individuals, and no two dates, are quite the same thing.

Still, dating can't be ignored. It is serious: it's the way most Americans come into romantic connection with the opposite sex. The way you think of dating probably affects the way you think of about half the world's population. The consequences are serious. Take this case:

> ▶ **What is love?** And how can you really know if you're in love?
>
> I have two friends, Brian and Denise. They have been going together for about 6 months. At the beginning of their relationship they agreed not to have sex, but by now they have sex regularly and often Brian's friends will walk in on them. Denise has no more self-respect and doesn't care who sees her.
>
> Last month she told me that she and Brian were madly in love and that she didn't want to be with anyone but him. Well, she's lived up to that. We used to be close friends, but now anytime I want to do anything with her she doesn't want to unless Brian goes too. Brian is the same with his friends. Both of them are Christians, but now they rarely come to church. They are planning to marry next year, but neither of them has plans for the future beyond that. They could care less about school, or about anything but each other. They are both very jealous of each other.
>
> Please tell me if this is love. I want to know because right now I don't have a boyfriend, so I can't know what they feel. If this is love, I don't want anything to do with something that would make me turn my back on my friends and make me jealous and selfish.

The answer is yes, that is love — one kind of love. Romantic, sexual love has this side: it can be selfish and jealous. It is also very unreliable: it can change faces in a day. The most beautiful girl in the world suddenly turns repulsive. The boy you wanted to talk with forever becomes someone you can't discuss the weather with.

Romantic, sexual love has another side, too: a very beautiful side of promises and joy and self-giving. The problem is how to bring out the good side and humanize the bad side.

110   *A Love Story*

The problem is not, as I see it, to stimulate romance. Our genes do that adequately. I have yet to see evidence that falling in love solves any problems, though it promises to take you directly to heaven.

So if you want to know how to fall in love or how to attract a partner, you are reading the wrong book. There are formulas, and I suppose some of them work. I suppose books on "How to Pick Up Girls" work, too. But I wonder if the end result isn't worse than what you started with. My only advice is to be yourself as much as you can, and if you are shy (which I am) be as courageous as possible. Most of all, remember that you are dealing with other human beings who probably are every bit as afraid as you, also wanting to fall in love every bit as much as you do. They aren't likely to reject you. Most people like most people.

Some help, huh?

Here are a few hints on how to humanize romantic love.

Make friends, not lovers. Becoming lovers will take care of itself. The most important thing is to become friends. One friend of mine made it a rule to never end an evening without having learned at least one important thing about the girl he was with, and having shared at least one important thing from his own life.

The main reason for going out ought to be getting to know each other. Therefore, your main activity shouldn't be making out, watching movies, eating expensive (or cheap) meals, or even having fun. The main activity should be talking.

Creativity helps. Building a bookshelf together on a Saturday is a cheaper and more helpful activity than sitting in a dark theater for two hours listening to someone else talk.

Often being in a group, or with another couple, is a much better environment for getting acquainted than the formal, tense problem of creating five hours of face-to-face conversation. No wonder so many turn to making out. It means they don't have to talk.

Stay balanced. Love wants to take over your life. It claims to be the only thing worthwhile, so couples often give up everything else, including outside friendships. But they usually discover that love by itself becomes too intense and too ingrown. Make a conscious effort to continue the rest of your life: other friends, other activities, time with God, time with family. Don't put them in competition with your romance, or you'll end up splitting yourself in two. And if the romance dies, you'll be left with nothing.

Resist infatuation. Love generally lies, trying to convince you that your partner is the only one in the world. He lies the most to people who haven't gone out much. As a rule, try to spend some time with other members of the opposite sex, *especially* when you feel those early waves of infatuation coming on. Dating someone else a time or two tends to provide perspective, but at the least, a long talk in the cafeteria with someone else will help.

Let commitments form naturally. It's natural to become more committed as the relationship grows. The trouble is, love pushes you into more than you're ready for. Making out increases your commitment. Be cautious of what you "say" with your hands. The same goes for saying things like "I love you." They're potent words. I think we ought to keep them as potent as possible by reserving them for very special cases.

And going steady? I don't see a need for any verbal agreement. "Going together" usually comes naturally in its own time. But why push jealously for it when at least one of you would just as soon still be experiencing more variety? Let natural selection lead you to "go together."

Don't hang on for security's sake. It's hard to break up a comfortable relationship and begin something new. But going out with a variety of people is invaluable experience, and few things are worse than nursing a relationship that's become boring and dead.

After things get weird and you split up, remember your responsibility to continue a loving friendship.

A Love Story

Should All Decisions Be Male-Made?

My girl friend and I have been arguing about something, and I'd like to get your opinion. When I first got to know her, I tried to have something planned whenever we went out. But that's beginning to feel stupid to me. We've been going together for a year and three months now, and I think she should be part of making decisions, too. In our town there isn't that much to do. If I just decide what we're going to do, I don't know if she likes it or not, and we can have a lousy evening because of it. In fact, we had a bummer last night. I asked her what she wanted to do, and she got mad. She said that was the guy's decision. I said she was old-fashioned, and that really made her mad. We argued, and never did go anyplace. Who's right?

YOU BOTH ARE. You're right that she ought to take part in decisions. A relationship goes two ways, and it's unfair to put the whole burden of designing an enjoyable evening on the guy's shoulders.

But your girl friend is right to get mad at you for showing up at her door and saying, "What do you want to do?" You should have made a decision at least a day in advance. When you plan ahead you can be more creative (for example, you can be dressed properly for catching frogs) and you don't sit around half the evening trying to decide what to do. You can concentrate on each other instead of the decision-making.

But there really isn't a "right" way to do it. Every couple is going to feel comfortable doing it a little differently — and no two people are going to agree totally. Consider it good "bending" exercise.

How Do You Know Love Is Real?

How do you know if love is for real? Helen and I have been together for two years. We're both seniors in college. We both want God's will for our lives, and naturally marriage is starting to come into the picture. We haven't talked about it, and I feel a lot of inner conflict. How do you really know?

$\backsim$ I WISH I KNEW. I don't. I don't think anyone really does.

Of course, there are some things you ought to check out. The advice of people you trust. The way in which you would serve God better together than separately. The completeness of your relationship: do you like each other? Can you laugh? Can you fight and then resolve the difference? Are you best friends, or does the physical attraction play too big a role? Are there subjects that you don't feel free to talk about? How mature are you — mature enough to face sickness? Poverty? Deep disagreement?

Only two things offer anything close to a guarantee: time and prayer. The longer you've been together, the more your love will have been tested. And prayer stakes everything on the idea that God is a loving Father who wants us to come to the right decision. I believe that as Christians you can trust Him to guide you to the correct decision. He probably won't do it through voices from heaven, though.

Any period of deciding is difficult. The only consolation is that it can build faith like almost nothing else. All the wisdom in the world couldn't know enough about the future to decide "intelligently." So you have to trust God. There's no other choice, really.

I simply believe that God will show you what He wants you to do at the right time — that if you're open to Him, you'll make the right choice. It sounds risky — and it is. But it works.

Love-Sick

Here's my problem, I will give all the facts I can.

1. I met this girl in my ninth-grade algebra class.

2. We became friends.

3. Then during the summer we ended up in driver's ed together, and I discovered what a wonderful person she is.

4. I wanted to take her out one night but she was dating this other guy.

5. *So, to make a long story short, it has been about one year and eight or nine months since I met her, and about a year of wanting to take her out.*

6. *I called her the other night at the suggestion of my best friend, and I found that she is dating another guy. I know this sounds silly, but I really got depressed. I've been turned down before, but I never went this low. I have been really praying about this for the last two months, but I have not received an answer. I really need her friendship. It has got me down and as a result I have not been able to eat as much as I should and have lost five pounds. Maybe I just have a hang-up?*

IF IT'S A hang-up, it's about the most normal one in the world. The names of those who share your feelings at this instant could easily fill the Manhattan telephone book. I can imagine several questions you're probably asking:

Why do I feel this way? Very simply, because you care for her, and you've been rejected. That does hurt.

If you wanted to avoid all pain, you could ask your parents to choose your marriage partner and then never speak to another girl until your wedding day. But assuming you prefer to choose your own romances, you have to expect rejection sometimes. As long as you're human, that will hurt.

How do I get rid of these feelings? Wait. They'll go away. In the meantime, cultivate an understanding of others who are depressed.

Is God trying to tell me something? It's possible. Probably He's telling you that right now this particular girl isn't the right one.

Should I keep trying? If you're willing to take the chance of continued rejection, why not? I'd only make two cautionary suggestions. First, don't bug her. She's chosen to go out with someone else for now, and if you respect her you'll respect that choice. God is capable of bringing you together in His own time if He wants. Concentrate not on "winning" her, but on being a friend who accepts her as she is — including the choice she's made. You'd be better off trying to get better acquainted in a nondating setting.

Second, take out someone else. The best way to nurture infatuation is to isolate it. Spending time with other girls will let in fresh air. If there's more to your feelings than infatuation, the first girl will outlast the competition. Otherwise — there are plenty of fish in the sea.

Giving a Guy the Bad Word

I *have known Rich for about three months now. He's part of a group of kids I'm in, and many times we all go out together for coffee. I like him as a friend, but I think he has a crush on me and I just don't feel that way about him. We've gone out a few times, but the last couple times he's called up I've begged off. Once I really was busy, and another time I had an excuse. But I could sense he was disappointed.*

I like him, and don't want to make him feel he's repulsive. But I would also like him to know that I don't feel romantic about him. How can I?

THERE ARE TWO ways to do it.

One is to string out excuses and act cold until he finally gets the idea. The other is to tell him directly, the next time he asks you out. I've heard it both ways myself, and I know which I prefer — the second way. Most guys feel the same. It hurts for a while, but you're not so involved you can't get indignant and forget it in a few days. The longer you wait, the harder it is for him.

→ Try something like this: "Rich, I like you a lot, and I enjoy being around you. I value you as a friend, and I don't want to lose that. But I get the impression I'm confusing you — you're thinking romance, and I'm not. So I think I ought to make it clear that's how I feel right now. Can we continue as friends?"

I'd tell him, too, how you feel about saying that. Tell him

A Love Story

you'd been afraid he'd take it wrong, but you decided he'd be able to understand without thinking it had something to do with not liking him.

Don't expect miracles. It will hurt him, though he probably won't let you know. He might act angry for a while. Sometimes the kindest thing, though, is to hurt someone a little — so you won't have to hurt him more later on.

This applies, by the way, to people who feel nervous because their partner is more serious than they are. It doesn't help to string him or her along because you don't want to cause pain. It's better to cause pain and get it over with.

Fear

A couple of years ago I liked this guy in my youth group. We started talking to each other, and were slowly developing a friendship. But just as we reached the high point of our relationship things began to change. He started dating another girl in our youth group. This hurt me deeply, and I couldn't understand. He was barely speaking to me. I didn't know what I had done to offend him.

Although I am still hurt, after much prayer and the Lord's help I have learned to accept the circumstances. But my problem now is that I'm afraid to like another guy. I'm shy anyway, and I was so thrilled to go out on my first date with this guy. Now anytime I start to like a guy I get scared. I don't want to get so excited and happy and then get hurt again. I know it's wrong to have this feeling of fear but I don't know how to stop it.

FIRST JOHN 4:18 says, "Perfect love casts out fear." The more deeply you understand God's love (and you never will fully understand it in this world), the further fear will be from your heart. His is the only perfect love.

There are good reasons for fear. This probably won't be the last time you'll be hurt by some guy. But being imprisoned inside yourself is worse than being hurt.

Read Romans 8:35-39, where Paul says, "Nothing can separate us from the love of Christ," and then goes on to list all kinds of horrible things, right down to death, which *fail* to cut us off from His love. That's not just an emotional, religious pick-me-up. It's very practical. If nothing can ever take away the love that really matters, why be afraid? A man who has millions in the bank doesn't worry much about pickpockets.

If you set your priorities so that you have time with God and other Christians, you'll find God's love for you sinking deeper into your mind and emotions.

You can't meet the fear you feel head-on — there's no talking yourself out of it. But you can ask God for the strength to continue to open yourself to guys, and to act fearlessly even when you don't feel fearless. When you do what you're supposed to, it's amazing how often the emotions fall into place by themselves.

In that context, you might think about the advantages of forming friendships with guys. It is an alternative to the hot-and-cold kind of romance you've just been through. The guy who dropped you probably didn't have a thing against you — he just didn't know how to handle his strong emotions of embarrassment and fear of having you cling to him. He wasn't strong enough to tell you how he felt and carve out a less romantic friendship with you. It might be, too, that you unintentionally made it hard for him to do that, by trying too hard for a romance that was already over. If you'd been good friends in the first place, it might have helped a lot.

Shy

I'm a very shy person. I would love to ask girls out, but I'm afraid to. Basically I don't know how, which may sound funny (it does to me), but it's the truth. I also have a problem with acne — not bad, but it bothers me. I feel terribly frustrated. I've talked to chaplains and psychiatrists. All they do is tell me what my problems are. I know what my problems are. I just don't know how to solve them.

A Love Story

I've prayed and I still don't seem to be getting anywhere. I'm just very lost and lonely. I have no one and I have no real friends. It's not that I'm not friendly; I am. In fact, I've been told that I'm overly friendly. How can a person be overly friendly?

I've talked with other Christians and asked them for help with my loneliness. They told me I wasn't alone. They said Jesus was with me. I know He is, but can He make me feel good when I'm down, or make me laugh when I'm sad?

I know God loves me, and I love Him very much, but I still feel very much alone. I have one dream and that is to have a family and a home to put them in. But I haven't even been able to get to first base.

Loneliness is my greatest fear. It seems I'm stuck with it.

THOUGH THERE AREN'T any instant solutions, I've known people who learned to cope with their shyness over a period of years. Progress comes one small step at a time, but it can come. And you're starting from the right place: with at least an intellectual understanding of God's love for you and your security in that. With that as a basis, you can develop the courage to reach out to people.

There's no substitute, though, for the brave act of approaching someone. I do know that there are many people who would be happy to get to know you. How do I know? For one thing, many have written me. There are many shy, lonely people. And nearly everyone feels lonely at times. Few people are in the position of turning away potential friends.

But I doubt if the right place to start is by asking girls out.

The right place to begin is, I think, to forget about other people filling your loneliness. Begin looking for people *you* can befriend. Look around you: aren't there people who are lonely? If you can't find them anywhere else, try a rest home.

It may be that those aren't the kind of friends you were looking for. You were hoping for someone who could help you — not someone in need of help. But how does that make you different from the people indifferent to *your* needs?

I got a letter a little like yours. A girl wrote,

▶ **I want many friends to go places with** and have a lot of fun with. I know you have to be nice but I've tried and I just can't be popular! I'm clean and people tell me I'm pretty. I also pray to make my life change, but nothing changes. Please help me, I want to have a fulfilling life!

In some ways it's both a funny and a sad letter. But do you see yourself in it at all? She's a little more obvious than most of us would be: "Please give me friends! Bundles of friends! Let me be admired! Let me be loved! I'm willing to pay the price; just name it!"

A Christian view of friendship must be different. We have to imitate our leader, Jesus Christ. Remember that He wasn't the most popular man who ever lived. He didn't spend hours trying to attract people to Him. Instead, He looked for the needs of people around Him. He was rewarded, not with vast popularity, but with a few close friends — and the approval of His Father in heaven.

For us, friends are not a "right." They are a "gift." What all of us are told to do is love others, and let the loving we receive rest in God's hands.

Aren't there lonely people around you whom you can love? I'm not promising this is easy, but you have to start somewhere. It could be a long road, and though you've tried chaplains and counselors before, I'd encourage you to try again. Some are better than others; some are better suited to your personality than others. Finding one who'll encourage you while you grow is worth many misfires.

Dating Non-Christians

I am a senior in high school. My boyfriend is a junior, and we have been going together for about two weeks. We really hit it off great together. I am a Christian, and though he isn't, he doesn't drink, smoke, take drugs, or go for sex before marriage.

But my mother gave me this big lecture about going with him. She thinks something is going to happen (like becoming pregnant). He told me that one of his sisters became pregnant before she was married and he never forgave her, so I know he doesn't believe in it. We don't plan to get serious because I will be going on to school (about 100 miles away), and he has two years more of *high school. We are just going together for this year. Please tell me your opinion. Do you feel there is anything wrong with going with him?*

THAT DEPENDS ON what "going with him" means. If it's as low-key as you say, then I think it's fine. Christians aren't supposed to isolate themselves from non-Christians; Jesus didn't, and He told us not to. A good, solid friendship could be a good experience for both of you. This one might have the particularly wonderful dimension of letting you introduce him to Jesus Christ.

However . . . (and here I gulp) there is a risk involved.

The risk is that you'll get head over heels in love, and won't be able to help yourself. Many people have experienced this. Here's one:

> ▶ **I've been dating a non-Christian since last August.** He knows of and respects my commitment to God, as well as my morals, but he does not share my beliefs. Our relationship has grown from a casual friendship into a deep love for each other. Now, as I consider the future, I realize what a step I was taking in deciding to date him. I can't marry him, for our relationship wouldn't be a Christian union dedicated to God. Yet, I am very serious about him. The result is one frustrated female, struggling with her emotions. The longer I wait, the less I want to give him up.
>
> I didn't intend to get involved. It happened before I realized it. I am afraid that I may someday choose to marry him despite knowing I shouldn't. I can only hope and pray that day will never come.

Experiences like that have led a great many wise Christians to conclude that Christians simply should not, ever, date non-Christians. I don't agree. I think it depends a great deal on the person, and on what he means by dating. But I'd caution you to think long and hard about yourself. Maybe your mom's concern comes from an intelligent observation of the way you are. If consciously or unconsciously you're thinking about getting seriously involved, it's dangerous. The emotions of "love" can sweep you into something that'll hurt you both — and I'm not talking about pregnancy. I'm referring to a deep bond of love although one party can't share an inner relationship with Christ.

If you do go ahead, I would caution you on a couple of other points. First of all, talk things over calmly with your mother. Bring your boyfriend over to meet her, so she can see the kind of person he is. And *keep* talking to her about how it's going between you and him. The odds are good that when she sees your positive, thoughtful attitude, she'll go along. If she won't, and she forbids you to see each other, I wouldn't fight it. She may be forbidding it because she understands you and the situation a lot more deeply than you do. At any rate, it's no great thing to sacrifice a yearlong, relatively casual friendship to build up a stronger lifelong relationship with your mother.

Also, you ought to be particularly conscious of problems with sex. Just believing it's wrong isn't enough: many unmarried mothers and fathers believed it was wrong. If it's really just a friendship, drawing the line early shouldn't be hard. Long, passionate kisses are hardly the kind of thing you do with someone who's just a friend.

But they're tempting, because we all have a strong sexual drive. You have the strength of Christ to resist that temptation. Your boyfriend doesn't, so your responsibility doubles. Though going with a Christian guy is hardly a guarantee that sex will be under control, the strain you experience going with a non-Christian is likely to be greater.

Perhaps more dangerous is losing contact with other Christians and ultimately God. This can happen in gradual, subtle ways. One person wrote me a long, sad letter about how it happened to her, and she closed this way: "You know what scared me the most about this whole thing? I went through all those changes (getting away from God) without even realizing it."

It can happen if your boyfriend takes up too much time, and doesn't want to go with you to Christian gatherings. Before you know it you're too busy to pray and spend time with other Christians. You're not reading the Bible. Naturally, you feel lost and lonely. But instead of turning to God and to other Christians, you turn even more to the guy. You stop talking to him about Jesus because your relationship with

Jesus isn't too great, and you feel hypocritical pushing it at him. And without planning it, you've drifted far from God.

What's the alternative? You have to work hard to maintain your own priorities in life. It's harder while going with someone who doesn't love God as you do. If you're not ready for that challenge — if you suspect there's more in this than "friendship" — if your mother won't go along — I'd cool it. There are more important things in the world.

What's Different About Non-Christians?

You seem to say that getting seriously involved with a non-Christian is dangerous. Personally, I think Christ was a fantastic person. He was filled with love. But I do not believe in God or in any superior being. Maybe my god is the feeling of love, but I hate to even use the word "god" because its connotation is a human-like thing guiding us, whom we must worship or else we will end up in "hell."

Now let me tell you, not all of us non-Christians are so beastly as you make us sound. I'm sorry if I sound angry, but your viewpoint sounds so narrow-minded. I can see that God and Christ mean an awful lot to you, and I respect that. But not everybody is alike.

I would be very hurt if somebody told my boyfriend that it was dangerous to go out with me because I am not a Christian. I don't like the idea that we classify people according to what they believe. We are all people and we all love each other, so what difference does it make?

THESE QUESTIONS ARE very good ones, raising points that often are a source of misunderstanding between Christians and non-Christians. I'll try to explain my point of view as clearly as I can.

In an odd combination, Christians believe that they are both exactly the same as everyone else, and completely different. To us, Christianity isn't just beliefs. Our faith is a living relationship with a person, and we find that He has changed us in a crucial way. Perhaps an analogy can help explain.

Suppose you're in Carlsbad Caverns, deep under the ground, when the lights go out. Everyone stumbles around, trying to find a way out, and the situation gets desperate. No one has a light. Finally, after several hours, a dim light far up the path comes on. You see it and shout, "C'mon, everyone. I see the way out!" But no one follows you. All they say is, "Sure you know the way. That's fine for you, but I don't see anything." And then in the dim light you notice that they have all reflexively closed their eyes in the dark. They don't realize it; they just think it's dark. When you tell them to open their eyes, they think you're insulting them.

On the one hand, you're no different from them. You're no wiser, no better physically or mentally, and the light is dim so you still bump into things. But you know where you're going, so in a sense you are totally different. You'd be a fool to do anything but leave the group and find your way out — assuming you couldn't talk them into coming with you.

That's what we Christians believe about ourselves. We've "seen the light" and are finding our way out. We're certainly no better than anyone else, and we certainly don't think we'll be contaminated by being friends with non-Christians. We have no right to be proud of ourselves — we didn't turn on the light. But our orientation in life — our values, our ideals, our goals — are completely different. We place that light above everything else. To become totally allied with someone whose eyes are shut to the light would just be stupid — and dangerous. We'd never find our way, and our alliance would be miserable, because we'd disagree about the most basic thing in life.

Christians believe that marriage is total — much more than friendship plus romance. Christian couples share their lives so completely they are almost one person. So, obviously, it would be a mistake for a Christian to marry a non-Christian. They would never really understand each other at the deepest level, never be totally united. It would hinder and confuse both of them. That's why the Bible says, in 2

Corinthians 6:14, "Do not be bound together with non-Christians."

Dating is another question. For some it's a hunt for a marriage partner, whether they admit it or not. They ought to stick to Christians.

Others are the type who fall easily in love — and they, too, would do well to stick to those who share their values. Those who are mature, and who are really looking for friendship — to whom dating is "just fun" — are free to date anyone they like.

Interracial Dating

I am a black girl trying very hard to do what's right. I have known this white guy in my school for five months now. He is one of the greatest guys I know, and we talk to each other a lot. Just last week some of his buddies told me he really likes me and wants to ask me out. I'm not sure he will, but if he does I want to be prepared and know what to do. I have searched through the Bible trying to find answers, but I haven't succeeded. I have spent much time in prayer, but still I have found no answers. What does the Bible say about whites dating blacks? There is nothing I want more than to please Christ.

THE BIBLE DOESN'T say anything about it. If offers no right or wrong in dating any person, and no restriction to marriage except between Christian and non-Christian. What the Bible does make clear is that the barriers between the races are broken down in Jesus Christ. There are differences in background and experience between races which you ought to consider. But in Christ you have complete freedom to choose whom you date.

Of course, it's only fair to point out that there is much pressure in society (and in church) against interracial dating and marriage. You do have to consider the static you'll both get. It puts a lot of pressure on you which bears thinking about ahead of time.

Whatever you do, don't date on the sly. You don't have to flaunt it, but trying to hide it would simply make you feel guilty. A double life is hard to live with. If you decide you want to date this particular guy, do it in the open.

A Love Story

7
Miscellaneous Topics

When Parents Don't Approve

Two years ago I met a guy at church. Wow! Could we talk! We really became close in a family-type relationship. But as time passed, my feelings for him took another turn. So did his for me. The last week before he left for college we were at camp together, and there we dedicated our relationship to God and asked His guidance for us.

But now when he comes home (about once a month) I can't date him because his mother disapproves. His parents are very strict. I'm not yet 16. He's 18, and can make his own decisions, but he respects his mother's wishes. I can understand how his mother feels, but is it fair? What should I do? It's tearing me up with worry.

ONE THING YOU can't do is live his life for him. He has to coexist with his parents for the rest of his life — and he's the one who must decide whether going with you is more important than upsetting them. I wouldn't try to unduly influence him, either — it could backlash on you. The most I'd try is this: try to get to know his parents better. Ask him whether he'd mind asking permission to have you over to dinner some night, to get to know them. Maybe when they see what sort of a person you are they'll feel differently.

All you can do, other than that, is let him know the feelings of doubt and frustration that worry you. But it's his life, so it's his decision.

That doesn't mean you have to let him decide about your life. If your boyfriend continues on his present course (which he probably will), then you can either mope around worrying about him, or you can hang him up for the present. I'd suggest the second possibility. It might help him to get motivated, and since any good times with him are in the future anyway, it would give you a chance to develop and grow with other people. That never hurts.

When Parents Interfere

I'm 15 and I guess my problem is common. I'm pretty sure I'm in love with a girl my age. We've been going together for about seven months, but my parents are really starting to give me hassles. They want me to go with other girls and are almost insisting. But I don't want them picking out girl friends for me. They think they're doing it for my own good, and they just laugh at me when I try to explain the love we have. They say there'll be many more after June. They also say they will stop letting me go out with her if I don't change something soon. How can I tell them to lay off? My mother is very Christian; you'd think she'd try to help instead of hurting.

I DON'T KNOW the answer to the generation gap. I know there is a gap, at least where "who to go out with" is concerned. It's natural to go through some problems while your parents (and you) are adjusting to your increasing independence. But that doesn't make the adjustments any easier.

What can you do? First, communicate. Parent-child conversations often consist of both sides putting up their nonnegotiable demands along with their most negative attitudes (expressed through grunts or body postures). Naturally, negotiations don't stand a chance. Try sitting down and asking questions. What are they worried about? What do they think of June? Try to explain calmly the way you feel: not "this is the way it is, or else," but "this is the way I feel; can you understand that?" Ask them if you could invite June over to meet them, not just to say hello, but to sit down for a meal or go along on a family outing. Get them talking to each other.

If June is as good as you think, and you're as mature as you think, your parents probably will come around. Maybe they'll at least agree to a compromise, where you do a few more things with your life than see her.

And what if they don't come around? Then I'd recommend you go along with them. Don't make speeches. Don't rant and rave. Just accept it as maturely as you can, with God's help.

There are several reasons for this. First, it's possible that, having been through a little more life than you, and having observed you since you were a little kid, they know something you don't. I'm not saying that's so; parents, even from good motives, make plenty of mistakes. But more often, I'd say, buried somewhere in that "no-you-can't" logic some parents get so fond of, is a good, common-sense reason. It might even be something they can't explain to you, but just see intuitively.

Another reason is that you have to live with your parents for a long time. In a few years you'll be on your own, able to date anyone you like: although at that point they might still disapprove, they'll probably recognize the natural limits to their control. But you'll still have to live with them. If psychology since Freud has taught us anything, it's that parent-child relationships are very important. They will affect you long after you've left home.

I believe it's worth some sacrifices to make sure those relationships are as good as they possibly can be. The more maturely you take those sacrifices, the easier it'll be on everyone. Besides which, you might just show enough maturity for your parents to realize they're wrong.

One other reason: the Bible has some strong language about obeying parents. I'm not one who believes you have to obey your parents after you've become an adult — though you should always respect and honor them. But I think there are many good reasons for obeying them as long as you're dependent on them. One of those reasons is simply that God says it ought to be that way.

Too Young to Marry?

I'm very confused and I don't want to make a mistake. I'm engaged to be married at the end of May. I truly love the guy and he truly loves me. We've gone to our church's marriage counseling, and he feels he is ready. He has a good job, and I have a part-time job along with my school classes. I'm afraid, though, that after I'm married I'll want to go out and see the world. I'm 16 *but will be 17 before we're married. He is 20 and tells me he'll help me grow up if we have problems. I want to marry him, but I'm unsure if this is the right time.*

RULES ARE MADE to be broken, but all the rules say it isn't the right time. The percentage of failure in teenage marriages is appalling. There is plenty of time to get married in a few years; why the big hurry? Especially when you're so unsure, you'd be absolutely crazy to let this guy talk you into marriage.

No guy at 20 is mature enough to help anyone else grow up. He's still got lots of growing to do himself — and the more he realizes it, the closer to being genuinely mature he is. Besides, a marriage is a partnership of equals — not a nursery in which one partner "raises"the other to his level. Don't do it! I do know of some teenage marriages that turned out all right. But they were very sure of what they were doing. And for every one of these successes, there are several failures who thought they knew what they were doing, but couldn't take the pressure.

Nudity Equals Pornography?

I *went to an art exhibit with my girl friend. There were quite a few nude paintings, which I didn't think anything of. But my girl friend is from a very strict background. When we'd been there only a little while she said she wanted to go. They really bothered her.*

We got into a big argument later on. I said I didn't see anything wrong with nude paintings, because they were art. She said there was no difference between those paintings and the centerfold in Playboy. *Who's right?*

PORNOGRAPHY, LIKE BEAUTY, is mostly in the eye of the beholder. Did you know that in Victorian England it was

A Love Story

common to put skirts on the legs of tables, to forestall "indecent" exposure?

At the other extreme is the famous film-maker Jean Renoir, son of the great French impressionist painter. His father often painted nude models at home when Jean was a boy. When he started school Jean was amazed to find the other boys looking at "dirty" pictures of nude women. He couldn't understand it. The pictures had no interest to him.

What's pornographic in one society isn't in another. Topless women are shocking in our society, but not in many primitive ones. Even that case gets more involved: in our society, a woman who breast-feeds her baby in public isn't tantalizing. The situation often determines whether something is erotic or not. If everyone is thinking "sex," it's stimulating. If people are thinking "motherhood" or "art" (as in a photo gallery), then it often is not sexually stimulating. It depends on 1) your background, 2) the circumstances, and 3) your own frame of mind.

So how do you find a workable definition of pornography that applies to everyone? The courts have been trying for years, and have just about given up.

However, an individual can make his own "Supreme Court decision" and stay away from what's unhelpful to him. Some things probably are bad for nearly everyone. Given what the skin magazines are trying to do, I doubt many could read them without tending to lose God's high view of sex. But other things — like a Renoir painting of a beautiful nude — do different things for different people. The artist wasn't thinking "lust" when he painted it. You don't think "lust" when you see it — you see a beautiful painting.

But it will disturb some people — notably your girl friend. Don't look down on that. Would you want someone from Pago Pago to look down on you because you can't see a woman's breasts without being turned on? The important thing is to protect each other from things that aren't helpful — doing it with a respectful attitude, and a willingness to bend your own pleasure to help someone else.

Which means, stay away from certain art exhibits when you're with your girl friend. There's no value in "liberating" her from her feelings. There is value in respecting her for who she is.

Meeting A Curfew

My dad makes me get home from a date by midnight, which I think is ridiculous. Many times I have to leave a party when it's hardly beginning. He says he doesn't want me to get into trouble, but I'm old enough to know what I want to do. If I decide I'm going to do something, I can do it before twelve as well as after twelve. The clock doesn't influence that. I know I'm supposed to obey, but do rules like this make any sense?

THEY WOULDN'T if everything you did was based on calm, rational decisions. But I doubt everything is.

One guy told me this story:

▶ **I was 150 miles from home,** and completely alone on the beach with this girl. No one in that area knew me. All the instincts of sex were there. At the time it seemed like making love would be perfect, wonderful. There was nothing stopping us. The only thing that held me back was the Christian teaching I'd had in church, from Campus Life, etc. That teaching didn't make much sense to me then, but it left a nagging doubt in my mind that wouldn't let me go beyond certain limits. It wasn't a rational thing, but now I'm very glad it was there.

That's one example of how decisions are influenced by things that don't fit a neat, logical equation. Sex drives aren't logical, and sometimes an "irrational" factor like a parental rule can help you deal with an "irrational" sexy situation. People have told me that parental rules they hated at the time saved them a lot of grief. They're grateful now.

Obviously, if you let yourself go for long periods of time in a dark, intimate atmosphere with a member of the opposite sex, a decision you made earlier about how far to go might get lost in the excitement. And many of those "intimate moments" come past midnight.

This is probably what your father has in mind. I'd imag-

A Love Story

ine he remembers some postmidnight experiences of his own, and would just as soon you avoid them.

What he may not understand is that times have changed, and there's more to do after midnight than make out. I'd recommend you sit down with him and explain exactly what you'd like to do after midnight, why you don't like leaving parties then, etc. (incidentally, if you haven't proven you know to get in at 12:00 when that's the set limit, don't expect him to trust you with more time). If he still won't bend — well, you'll live. It's just possible your dad knows you better than than you know yourself, and has made a helpful rule.

Should I Tell All?

A while back I thought I was in love. We were both Christians and talked of marriage, though there were no definite plans. We slipped into petting and finally intercourse. By the time we reached that stage I had rationalized things, believing that since we were both Christians and did plan to marry eventually it was all right.

Not long after problems began, and finally he broke our relationship. It was the best thing for me. I see that now. As Christians we sometimes think we are exempt from God's rules or Satan's temptations. Sometimes when the Lord tells us what is wrong we don't understand why. I didn't realize this would affect me psychologically. Since that time I've asked myself, "Did he really love me? Was it real love or lust? Was he using me?" It has caused me to hate myself, and I know that I repulse this young man even though I've apologized. It has been three years since our relationship.

About six months ago I met a wonderful guy who really loves me, and whom I deeply respect. We plan on being engaged in late July. A while back he told me that if he were going to make the moves on me he would have done it, but he didn't believe in that. He said, "If I ever tried and you gave in I would lose respect for you." Having never had sex himself, he thinks that most people do it just for fun, that they are sluts or whores or loose women, etc., that they don't even think of the consequences.

Well, I don't think of myself as a slut, and I did think about the physical consequences (pregnancy, VD, etc.), but I thought I'd be careful. At the time I believed our love made it right.

Anyway, I have been forgiven by the Lord, and though I wish I could take back what I've done, no amount of wishing will erase the fact. But since I do hope to marry John, I feel we must have an honest relationship. But how honest? Should I tell him about my past life and risk losing him? Does he have a right to know?

I FAVOR THE total honesty route. If you're thinking seriously about marrying someone, it's to his and your own good to get things out in the open. There's risk in that — he'll probably be disturbed, and yes, you do risk losing him. But if his love goes very deep, it'll overcome the shock.

Holding secrets in isn't very pleasant. It's likely that sooner or later they'll come out, or he'll figure things out. Then he'll feel as though he's been tricked, and the marriage will seem like a trap. Even if he doesn't find out, you have to live with the fear that he might — and the knowledge that you're holding out. This kind of mental set isn't recommended for forming a good marriage.

I wouldn't encourage anyone to get carried away with honesty. There's no need to compulsively dish out details. It's enough for him to know that you went all the way, and why. Curiosity beyond that, though natural, isn't healthy. One man who'd led a very loose life before becoming a Christian in high school told his wife this: "Whatever you can imagine, anything you think of, just assume I've done it." He didn't feel it would be helpful to go into detail. I agree.

Nor do I think you're wise to confess to many people. Some evidently are so "honest" they tell all on their first date. I don't think that's helpful, either to you or to the person you're with. It's bound to make your past the focus of the evening, when the focus ought to be on your present.

The only people who need to know are those who are affected. If you're thinking about marriage, an entirely open relationship is important. If something still bothers you, then

A Love Story

for your own good, and the good of your relationship, it ought to come out.

Oral Sex

My parents didn't tell me about sex. I went out and read books and magazines. Naturally I learned about oral sex along with the rest of it, and accepted it. When the topic came up at home my mother was shocked to think I thought it was okay. She said no Christian would ever ask me to do such a thing. Since then I have noticed that in Christian circles when they tell young people about sex they never mention it except to say that anything outside regular sex is perversion. I wouldn't ask them about it lest they think I'm perverted.

THE BIBLE SAYS nothing about oral sex, so it seems to be something left to the individual. I don't know of any Christian writers on sex who find anything wrong with it, as long as it's within marriage and pleasurable to both partners. Outside marriage, I believe it's little different from the complete intimacy of intercourse, and thus out of bounds.

Copping Out on Marriage

Last spring I ended a relationship I'd had for three years. I felt we both needed to meet new people and find out how we really felt. Well, after doing this something happened. I met a Christian guy who simply swept me off my feet. I married him eight months later in a beautiful church wedding. Everything was perfect, I thought. I had finished a year and a half of college and I thought I knew myself. But I didn't.

No one could be as perfect as Fred. Everyone loved him. They couldn't say enough about him. I loved him too, but now I know it wasn't true love.

I left Fred three weeks ago. I'm not copping out on marriage; I *don't mind doing housework and cooking. We went out a lot and had a nice home in the country. I am sort of young (19), but that wasn't it either.*

My problem is that I still love my first boyfriend, and it's the deepest kind of love. He feels the same. (I never went out on Fred — I'm not that kind of person.) The problem I'm facing now is God. Will He forgive me? I have hurt so many people. I've been told I will pay for what I've done. I'm so afraid, but not afraid enough to go back to Fred. I know that God forgives and that no sin is greater than another. But I am so afraid of how God will make me pay for what I have done.

YOU MAY PAY for what you've done, but it won't be the way you think. God loves you, and He wants you to be joyful and calm. He doesn't want anything you've done in the past to disrupt your relationship to Him. But to have that relationship with Him, you have to do things His way. If you ignore Him, you'll be left alone to live with what you've done.

What *have* you done? You say you're not copping out on marriage, which evidently means cooking and cleaning to you. That's where you're wrong. It's understandable that your feelings toward your husband changed, and that marriage to him wasn't exactly what you'd expected. But allowing those feelings to run your life (and your husband's) is precisely what copping out on marriage is.

You've said, in so many words, that love is something that happens to you. It's either there or it isn't (and in your case, you thought it was but it really wasn't). Love isn't something you decide on; it decides on you.

That's usually true of falling in love, but marriage is many steps beyond falling in love. Marriage is the point at which you take control.

Many people think a wedding ceremony is a pleasant formality — kind of like the handshake that seals a bargain already made. Actually, a wedding ceremony should be a sign of a radical change in your relationship. Before it, most lovers feel "lost in love." But the wedding ceremony is more sober than that. You make a solemn, legal promise in front of practically everyone you know and love. You're saying, in

A Love Story

effect, "I may be crazy in love, but I'm still capable of choosing my own destiny. I haven't lost my mind. I have decided that, come what may, this person is the one I am going to love. I don't believe that God would allow me to make the wrong choice in something this important. This is a promise, and I will keep my promise."

That promise is closer to the true meaning of marriage than feelings of love are. Feelings come and go. A promise is something that stays the same forever.

That promise is the only thing stable enough to build ever-deepening love on. Such love requires a foundation to build on — the promise should be the unshakable foundation.

There's a good analogy in Watergate. We choose a president through the most elaborate, costly, lengthy procedure imaginable. The whim of every voting adult in America is counted, trying to find the right person for the office. Compared to this process, the way most people pick a husband or wife is like taking numbers from a hat.

But at the basis of his presidency is a promise: the inaugural promise he makes to carry out the law. His own feelings about what would be a good way to rule the country are always limited and controlled by that promise. When that promise is disregarded, tragedy results, as it did with Richard Nixon. Things fall apart, and it seems as though no one can trust anyone.

The same is true with you. Being careful about choosing a husband was important — and by your own account, you found a wonderful man. Once you've chosen, though, your promise becomes the center of your relationship — not how you feel.

The road to joy is to turn around and go back to your husband. Christians disagree whether divorce is allowable for Christians. But nearly all agree that divorce should come, if at all, only after you have fought tooth and nail to live up to your promises. It's obvious you haven't even begun doing that.

No doubt going back sounds impossible. With your feelings the way they are now, it probably is impossible. But our God can do impossible things.

You do need help from a trained, professional counselor who can help you through this. Your minister can probably recommend one if you don't know one.

You'll also need help from God. God wants to help you with your feelings. It is amazing how He can change them. When you act the way you should, asking Jesus to help, the feelings come.

Abortion

I was pregnant at 17 and had an abortion. I had it for several reasons. 1) My mother didn't want my sisters finding out about it. 2) I was so mixed up, I was willing to do as mother wanted. 3) I knew I couldn't have a baby right then. For one thing, I was still going to school, and wanted to finish without having to walk around seeing myself growing bigger and bigger, and see the other students' eyes on me. Also, I was sure mother would have made me give it up for adoption, which I couldn't have done after seeing my own beautiful child, so much a part of me.

People probably think of me as a stupid, inconsiderate bitch. To me, it's past, and the past is long gone, even though the painful memories remain.

Yes, maybe I've made a very big mistake, but I know that I'm not alone in that. Do you think that what I did or how I felt was wrong?

FOR ME, ABORTION takes away human life. Therefore it ought to be avoided at almost any cost. Convenience or shame isn't enough motive. I see the dangers in this position — I don't like the thought of more unwanted children in the world, especially children raised by mothers far too young. But it is my conviction that human life is sacred, and godly people will protect it as much as they possibly can.

But it is not in my interest, or God's, to condemn you. I have no taste for making loud proclamations against a sin I have never (and will never) be tempted to commit. And I believe God is more interested in putting the past behind than even you are. He wants to love you, and receive your love in return.

Birth Control

My girl friend and I are soon to be married. Our question is about the use of contraceptives. As Christians we should trust the Lord for everything, including when to have children. There is always risk when going on faith – is using no contraceptives an unreasonable risk? Or should we use them until the Lord says we are ready for kids?

USE THEM. We ought to trust the Lord to give us our daily bread, but that doesn't mean we shouldn't establish a set mealtime.

What Does the Bible Say?

I need some help on where in the Bible I could find verses that talk about the wrongness of premarital sex. My friends say it really depends on how you interpret the Bible. If you are able to help I would really appreciate it.

TRY 1 THESSALONIANS 4:3-8; Mark 7:21; and 1 Corinthians 6:12-20. There are others, but these are among the clearest.

Are there different ways of interpreting these verses? There are different ways of interpreting anything. The word translated in various versions as "sex sin," "immorality," or "fornication" is the Greek *porneia*, which generally means sexual intercourse between two unmarried people. There's no doubt in my mind, or in the minds of most biblical scholars, that there were only two alternatives Paul and Jesus endorsed: marriage or celibacy.

Usually people attack that statement by asking whether it's relevant to our day. They say what was condemned in the Bible was lustful, unloving sex, usually with a prostitute. No option like "living together" existed. And since Jesus offered love as the ultimate commandment, the argument goes, He would have thought loving sexually with some commitment was fine.

We do have to recognize one point: two people who love each other and live together without the permanent commitment of marriage aren't the same as two people who end up in bed for an evening, hardly having known each other and not expecting to see each other again. (See Matt. 19:3-12.)

But does "love" make it perfectly okay? No. In the first place, Jesus didn't set up "love" as being opposed to the rules God had given, but as fulfilling them. The rules still stood; if anything, they were broadened. And the model of marriage Jesus refers to, quoting from Genesis, is more than a feeling. It is a commitment. It is an institution bounded by rules. He puts it up as a high standard — so high the disciples ask Him "How can anyone be married?" But the only alternative He cites is celibacy. (See Matt. 19:3-12.)

Premarital sex, or "living together," may be loving and sincere, but it doesn't measure up to the full standard — and delight — of what God has given us in marriage. It's a poor substitute, and God has always warned us away from substitutes.

Is God Trying to Punish Me?

Bill, *my boyfriend, met me three years ago. Our love has been a very slow, building one — we didn't press it to happen. We didn't even start holding hands until the second year we knew each other, and we made our kissing a sacred sort of thing to be done only on special occasions. I feel our relationship has been great because of this. It also makes me realize that Bill honestly does*

A Love Story

love and care for me; he hasn't been going with me this long just to "get something out of me" like lots and lots of guys. Bill is a great Christian, and from his talking to me, pushing me and being patient with me, I have also come to know the love God has for me. I know from experience that God is the only one who can give me the real peace I need. I feel also that God gave Bill to get the message across, because I would never listen to anyone else.

Both Bill and I have agreed, a little reluctantly, to go out with other Christian kids and really get to know them. We both know that is the way our parents would like it, and we don't want any trouble with our parents. We both love each other, and we also realize God can keep our love growing. We would like very much to get married later . . . a lot later! We talked it over and decided that if we do get married it will be best after we have graduated from college. We don't want to really plan into the future, because we know God will do that for us.

We never even did any petting until about four weeks ago. Bill came over to "watch TV," but we didn't watch TV. We started kissing, then hugging, petting – and finally sexual intercourse. After, we were both shocked and ashamed of ourselves. We got down on our knees and prayed for a long time. But when I got up, the usual peace and love wasn't there. I felt more upset about it than ever!

Since then, we've hardly held hands. Bill says God has given him strength and forgiveness. But it seems like God won't forgive me! We kept praying about it, but God has not answered yet. I gave up praying altogether because I don't understand.

Now, a month later, I'm having all the signs of pregnancy. Bill keeps praying about it, and is trying to help me, insisting that God loves me and turning to Him is the only way. But I have given up. I am frightened with this new discovery of possible pregnancy, and there is no one to help me but God. But He won't! I've got an appointment to go to a family planning center, and if the tests are positive I will have to go back and have an abortion. Bill keeps praying, and trying to get me to pray too. I need more than Bill's love and concern. I need God's peace and forgiveness! I have almost completely given up as the days are going by and I keep gaining weight, waking up every morning sick, and other signs of pregnancy keep coming. Doesn't God care about me and love me *any more? Is He trying to punish me? I need God's help so much, but He's not there any more.*

WHAT CAN I say? What can anyone say? Only that you are not the first to go through such agony, and that God does let many of us suffer. He let His Son suffer too. The Bible is full of stories of people who loved God and yet were killed or persecuted or ridiculed. He does not pluck Christians out of this world of pain. We are a part of it, and have to live with cause and effect like everyone else.

What can you do? Twist your emotions into a lie and smile and give thanks? I don't think so. More than anything else, you are called to endure. God wants you to outlast the pain. He doesn't ask you for the impossible: to be happy when there is nothing to be happy about. (Sometimes He gives that kind of peace, but it is His gift, not something you can manufacture for yourself.) He wants you to wait. If you wait, you will find Him. You will survive this awful time, and new life will come. The old will fade away.

All you can lean on are His words. He has promised to never leave or forsake us. He is there, holding you, though you cannot feel Him. Don't try to make yourself feel His presence; just believe, and wait. He has promised that He will forgive those who are sorry, so He has already forgiven you. You don't have to feel it for it to be true. But you can begin to believe it, and stop beating yourself.

You want, no doubt, for Him to give you a miscarriage. Perhaps He will, but more likely He won't. Jesus came into the world, taking on our troubles. He has left us here, not telling us to escape, but to overcome those troubles with His help. Our thumbs still bruise when we smash them. Angry words still make us hurt. Intercourse still leads to pregnancy, which leads to babies and painful decisions. But the difference is that He loves us, forgives us and is with us, whether we feel it or not.

Married In God's Eyes

A Love Story

I *understand that sex is God's gift, beautiful inside the bounds of marriage and definitely wrong outside. I am a Christian guy, and I believe in what God says.*

But I have gone all the way many times, always with the same person: my fiancée. Our love is definitely real: the forever-love the Bible speaks of. We don't make love for lust. To us it is definitely an expression of our love.

I don't doubt that it would have been better had we waited until after marriage, but the Bible says that in God's eyes we are married right now. If we definitely are going to stick it out, it hasn't hurt our feelings toward each other, and we are already married in God's eyes, so why is it wrong for us to continue?

I HEAR THIS often: "The Bible says when you've had sex you're married in God's eyes." I have a problem with that: I can't find it in my Bible. It's ironic, really, how it's being used. I suspect it was originally used as an alternative to a shotgun in motivating guys to marry girls they'd gotten pregnant: "In God's eyes you're married, and marrying anyone else later will be adultery. So you had better formalize the deal with the justice of peace. Quick." Now it's shifted, as fuzzy interpretations of the Bible tend to, and is used as justification for premarital sex: "In God's eyes we're married. The ceremony is just a formality."

It's true that Exodus 22:16 says a man who seduces a virgin should marry her, or alternatively, if her father refuses to consent, pay the father a fine equal to the amount he could have expected had the girl married under normal circumstances. To me that's clearly meant to protect a woman's rights in a time when a nonvirgin couldn't expect anyone to want to marry her, and so would either have to be supported by her father the rest of her life or become a prostitute.

Another passage frequently cited for this argument is 1 Corinthians 6:15-17, in which Paul says, "Do you not know that the one who joins himself to a harlot is one body with her? For He says, 'THE TWO WILL BECOME ONE FLESH'" (NASB).

That means, very clearly, that sex is not simply a physical thing. Intercourse involves the total person. Paul is answering certain people in the church in Corinth, people suggesting, as some suggest today, that sex is a natural drive just like hunger. Paul says no. He says when you go to bed you mold yourselves together. He suggests that sex brings a spiritual unity whether you want it to or not. Therefore, sex outside marriage must be taken seriously.

But because you're "one flesh" doesn't mean you're married, in God's eyes or anyone else's. If that were so, the logical step for the Christians living in Corinth would have been to find the prostitutes they'd slept with and drag them to the altar. Paul doesn't suggest that. He instructs them to quit their sexual activity.

The conditions of marriage are broader than one flesh. They are quoted many times in the Bible: "A man shall leave his father and mother, and shall cleave to his wife; and the two shall become one flesh" (Matt.19:5, NASB). That gives two factors besides sex: totally committed, sharing love (cleaving), and a geographical, financial, and public (or legal) new beginning for the couple.

One other interesting passage is Jesus' confrontation with the Samaritan woman at the well (John 4:1-38). She was a woman with loose sexual morals. Jesus says to her in verse 18, "You have had five husbands; and the one whom you now have is not your husband" (NASB). He makes a distinction between her past husbands and the man she lives with. According to Him, being married and merely living together aren't the same.

When you've publicly and legally committed yourselves to each other (with no back door to keep open "in case I need to run"), when you're living together full-time, when you're financially working together (putting your money where your mouth is means more commitment than you might think), when there are no secrets to hold from each other or from friends, church, or parents, then the conditions for forever-love are optimum. And that's what marriage is all about. The results of *not* being committed to those optimum circumstances are pretty obvious in our society, don't you think? They could easily turn out to be obvious in your own relationship.

How can I stop lusting? It's especially bad when I'm at the beach, or when I see girls who are obviously braless. A wave of desperate feeling comes over me, and I can't think of anything but sex. It makes me very depressed.

A GUY IN California told me this: "Usually lustful feelings are the biggest problem when I'm feeling needy." That made sense to me: when I feel sorry for myself I'm most subject to seeing women as objects, and then the dehumanization and guilt pushes me farther into introspection. It's a cycle I have a hard time breaking out of.

If a car is out of tune, someone who knows auto mechanics can hear it. All the parts may be working perfectly, but if the timing is wrong, the engine fights against itself. When you turn the distributor and set the timing, suddenly the engine smooths out and starts to sing.

I find being thankful a little like that. Thankfulness seems to be the healthiest attitude I can have. When I thank God for my life it puts me "in tune."

So when I'm feeling needy, I try to be thankful. When I see a girl who's attractive, I don't try to pretend she isn't. I smile and say to myself, "Thanks, God, for making women attractive, and this one in particular. Help me to have a healthy, good-humored attitude toward her."

8

A Love Story

Had God consulted me about it, I should have advised him to continue the generation of the species by fashioning human beings out of clay, as Adam was made.

Martin Luther, *Table Talks*

Some Christians may wish that God had stuck with making angels; but God was delighted to have body-persons.

Lewis Smedes, *Sex for Christians*

Up until now this book has been, I hope, practical. People usually aren't interested in long-winded theorizing about sex.

People want answers on sex, as specific as they can get them. Starting with "How are babies made?" they proceed to "How far should we go?" "How do you know if you're really in love?" "How big are sexual organs supposed to be?" "What's the secret of a good marriage?" and so on. I've noticed, however, that specific answers, though they may temporarily safisfy, don't necessarily solve problems. Give me a person who doesn't know the specific answers but has a good attitude toward himself and others, who respects sex as something essentially sacred and wonderful, and I'll take him any day over the person stuffed with rules about whether to kiss on the first date and where the line of lust lies. They'll both have problems, but the first person will have some ways of solving them, and in the long run usually will come out all right.

The way you think about sex is very important.

If I set out to find the least controversial statement I could make on any subject, I think I would end up with this one: "Sex is good." No one disagrees. From the moment you first noticed that the opposite sex had grown attractive, you've known you were dealing with something life would be much duller without. Of course, when your body began to change during puberty, and when your mind first began to be preoccupied by the girl or guy in the third row of Mr. Scloett's class, it may have scared you. Sex was something even your parents weren't in control of: it was leading a revolution in your body without asking approval. But unless you had a rough childhood, it wasn't an unpleasant revolution. It was exciting, and it's continued to be.

This is in complete agreement with the biblical view. There are religions that think of the body and its sexual impulses (or food impulses, or need for sleep) as hindrances to spirituality. Some Christians, I'd have to admit, act like this too. But they're wrong. The Bible never separates your body from the rest of you. If you're going to be spiritual, you'll be spiritual in your body, just as Jesus was. In heaven you'll walk around in your body — a better one, but still a recognizable contraption. The Old Testament Jews were very earthy people. They didn't glorify the body as some Greek philosophers did — probably no one who lives by farming and herding has time to sit around thinking of the Body Beautiful as some sort of ideal. The practical man puts his body to work. But he respects it, and likes it, and is proud of it. That's the Jewish attitude, which also is the Christian attitude. It's reflected from the beginning of creation: when God made Man — corpuscles and muscles, bones and kidneys, penis and vagina — He congratulated Himself. He was pleased with what He had made.

What He had made was sexy. Adam was attracted to Eve. Presumably Eve was attracted to Adam. When they fell into sin, their first reaction was to cover their bodies, so the other (and perhaps God) couldn't see it. They became ashamed of and protective of their beautiful bodies. Ever since, healthy-minded men and women have shown their bodies only in the most private of circumstances, to the people they trusted the most. Primitive Indian tribes may go around nearly naked, but there is usually something — a loincloth, perhaps — which isn't needed for warmth, protection, or comfort. It protects their "private parts."

I believe modesty is Christian. In the kind of world we live in, we can't afford to be totally naked, physically or psychically, with everyone: we're too easily hurt and dehumanized. But where it's possible and appropriate, taking off your clothes and sharing your body with another human being, in love, is as beautiful as anything God ever thought of. It can be a bit of Eden. Sex is wonderful, and there are no apologies or stammered reservations to that. One whole book of the Bible — the Song of Solomon — is dedicated to naked love. If you read it hoping to be turned on, you'll be disappointed. But try to find a piece of literature more rapturously, delightedly prosex at the local drugstore. You won't.

Sex is good. Our bodies are something to be proud of. If we went no further, we'd end up exhibitionists. Animals go naked; why shouldn't we? Animals have sex in public, when the mood moves them; why shouldn't we? Why not discard the shame civilization has surrounded sex with?

Christians should be, I think, in agreement about discarding the shame. But shame is sometimes confused with protection. Some things are worth keeping private because they're so close to me that I lose part of myself if they're abused. My feelings about prayer are similarly protective. I wouldn't pray out loud in a bus station, not because I'm ashamed of my relationship with God, but because it's too personal. The same with sex. Sex is more than just my body. At this point, Christians begin to lean away from the quasi-scientific view of sex that is common today. We say that sex is a mystery, meaning that it is deeper and more complex than anyone will ever fully understand. It needs to be handled with great care.

But then, this isn't so difficult an observation to make. I don't believe this because "the Bible says it." I believe it because it's obvious. First of all, sex is very personal. I can shake hands with innumerable strangers and not feel cheap, but sex isn't that casual. Being rejected by the opposite sex hurts so badly because more than your body has been turned down. *You* have been rejected. Everything you stand for has been held up to examination and thrown aside. No matter how many times you've been through the romantic cycle, it's still painful.

And the more personal sex gets, the better it gets. If this weren't true, prostitution would be an enviable profession. As is, it's pitiable. The Happy Hooker may write books about its glories, but no one really believes her. We want sex because we want to be personally involved with someone we love in the deepest way possible. We want others to find us erotically attractive, but no one who's had the experience wants to be simply a sex object. We want to be sexy people, but more than that, we want deep personal intimacy. We want to take off the wraps and expose ourselves to someone we can trust to love us. We are animals who make love face to face.

And sex is spiritual, because men are spiritual. Even those who don't believe in God have to admit that men, unlike animals, find a place for God in their lives. When archaeologists dig up civilizations they find religion as much or more than government. The priesthood is as old a profession as prostitution. It is basic, and urgent, for men to worship God. Villages in medieval France whose people lived in cold, thatched-roof homes with dirt floors built, without machines, the most wonderful buildings ever made to the glory of God — the cathedrals. People who claim a starving man can't believe in a loving God are simply wrong: religion has never been a luxury.

But what can we mean when we say that sex is spiritual? After all, we don't want to do it in church. No one sings hymns while making love.

I mean that sex touches us in the same way God touches us. People who fall in love experience something they could almost call conversion. The similarities are more than superficial. Real love makes you very humble: how could this wonderful person love me? What does she see in me? You become conscious of your faults. And then you ask, how can I serve her? How can I do what's right by her? And beyond that, you feel as though she has changed you: somehow your relationship to her has made you feel almost regal, in a humble sort of way. When you're in love is almost the only time you ever feel like a king's (or a priest's) rich, flowing robe might fit.

Of course, these same things happen to those who meet God. He affects me in the same way she does. He also leaves me awed. Both kinds of love bring the strongest sense of holiness. It is no accident that we use the same word to describe both how we feel toward God and how we feel toward a lover: "love."

Of course, sex always brings us back to earth. (So does God.) We do sex with our bodies — awkward, funny-looking things in most cases. And sex is an embarrassingly constant part of our lives: we are sexual people when we are brushing our teeth, when we're working, when we're in church praying. It's not a once-in-a-while ecstatic experience; it's a constant experience that once in a while reaches ecstatic forms of expression. (So should religion be, of course.)

And this brings in another dimension: your mind. You have to make up your mind how you're going to use sex. There are constant choices.

This isn't as popular an aspect of sex, but everyone

knows and respects it. You don't act out every sexual whim: that's rape. And it's not just that you would hurt another person. People don't masturbate in public without getting carted off for psychological examination. Sex experts can rail against our sexual repressions, but they had better not suggest that the cure is to live by our animal impulses. The world would fall apart — we would become much less than human — if we always did what we felt like sexually.

Notice that we aren't really like animals at all. Most animals are not sexual all the time. You can put a male and female dog together full-time, and only during a small fraction of their lives will they treat each other sexually — when the female is in heat. When that time comes, as anyone who has kept dogs knows, sex is completely compulsive. No dog ever decided to have sex.

But we have a heavier burden. God has made us so we have to use our minds, and exercise our will. There is no getting around this, no matter what your ethical standards are like. Sex involves the mind. It involves choosing how to act, every moment of the day.

Of course, it also involves our minds in encountering another person, because, as I already said, sex is personal.

What else is sex? I have to take up some aspects of sex that are more controversial. First, sex is transactional. Something happens between partners. One person gives a part of himself to the other. Something is communicated. You aren't the same afterward. We express this in common language by saying a girl "gave herself" to someone else. The Bible uses the word "knew": Adam "knew" his wife. Sex is a way of saying something, and the more that's said the better. Prostitution is prostitution, but it is less than making love was meant to be.

I go further. Sex is the act that expresses total unity between two people. It helps create the unity, too. Naturally, total unity is restrictive — you can't give all of yourself to two people at once. And people don't like the restrictive clauses. But though they may not like them, sex does. It flourishes in security. It needs privacy. And it naturally makes promises: "I'll never leave you. I'll always love you." Sex, you see, wants more than physical pleasure. It wants total intimacy.

But there can't ever be total intimacy where you're unsure of tomorrow. You don't tell secrets today that your confidant is going to blab everywhere tomorrow. Only a commitment which binds you together forever is total.

I have to admit that marriage is a funny invention. One friendship is better than none, but two are twice as good. So why shouldn't two marriages be better than one? Why should I be limited to expressing my sexuality this way with one woman? Why not two? Why not one when I'm young, one when I'm raising children, and one when I'm old?

There are many answers which are quite practical. One is protection. Any total commitment must extend forever, or it will always be hedged. We simply can't live in commitment "minute by minute." We need reassurance about the future. Now that divorces are easy, and "living together" arrangements have lost their glamor, we're beginning to see more of the pain that results from less-than-totally committed love in a marriage.

Part of the answer has to be this, too: that sex is simply that way. It binds two people together totally — it is meant to, anyway, and when it's used in a situation where commitment is incomplete there are kickbacks. Sex is the totally personal action, implying total giving of yourself. Anything short of that shortchanges sex.

Perhaps I can put it positively. Gratitude demands marriage be singular. The Bible says that when God introduced Eve to Adam, Adam was happy and grateful. There had been a sense of incompleteness when he met all the animals, but finally he'd met someone like himself. And it is not recorded that he asked for more. One was enough! Only greed — and a lack of appreciation — would have made him want more.

This is the way it is with anything really "big." Wanting more than one is simply gluttony. The healthiest way is to choose one person and develop your relationship. Marriage is "big" enough to offer infinite variety — you don't have to ever be bored.

That, of course, is an idealistic view of marriage. One problem is that it often fails. Marriage often is attacked for the precise reason that it has left many people unhappy. Children of unhappy marriages, now grown up, wonder if it is worth sticking through a bad marriage "for the sake of the kids." They've seen too many marriages that ended in bitterness and divorce. They suspect marriage itself may be the cause of it, because it's so rigid.

Christians who are honest have to admit many of these criticisms. Marriages do fail. Of course, some of what are called marriages might never be called Christian marriage — but Christian marriages fail, too.

The only question I ask is, "What's the alternative?" Perhaps I could paraphrase a political saying: "Marriage is the worst possible living arrangement — except all others." And I might suggest that marriage, as a set of laws and an institution, isn't worth straw by itself, any more than democracy would be worth anything in a land of idiots or crooks. The rules and institutions can shape and encourage only what's there between two people. They can't manufacture it. Christians suggest that a good marriage is big and wonderful enough to be worth the effort. If many — even most — fail, does that mean the ideal ought to be discarded? Not unless another way proves to work better. Since God has given us marriage as our focus of sex, we feel confident that nothing will be better. In thousands of years of civilization, nothing better has yet turned up.

In Ephesians 5, Paul makes it clear that marriage, the Christian focus of sex, is a metaphor for the relationship of God to His people — a profound metaphor that we will never exhaust.

This doesn't mean, I think, that people will grasp great new truths about God through orgasmic ecstasy: that somehow God "reveals" Himself especially to those who are married. Some of the Greek religions taught this: that in having intercourse with the temple prostitutes, you were in effect "knowing" the gods. Some Christians talk about experiencing the divine wholeness of marriage as though it were an elite experience which enables them to learn something about God.

Jealous. We learn, first, what the Old Testament means when it says that God is a jealous God. Jealousy isn't an attractive emotion, and it seems odd to describe God with the word. But we understand jealousy in a marriage — we would consider it strange if a husband whose wife cared more for other men didn't feel hurt and anger. God wants us in a completely intimate relationship, and He knows we must give up other things to have that relationship.

In moving toward marriage, a person makes sacrifices. He gives up things that are in themselves good. A guy may give up spending so much money on clothes, in order to save money for marriage. A girl may give up the picture she kept as a symbol of a bygone relationship with someone else. The clothes aren't wrong. The picture isn't wrong. But to focus complete commitment on one person, distractions have to go. So it is with God. We must have a "single eye" toward Him. He is "jealous" until we do.

Trinity. Marriage teaches us something about the Trinity — how three persons can be one God. We mustn't stretch this — in marriage two persons are emphatically two persons, always — they don't lose their identity. But there is, or ought to be, a unique oneness about them. They become more than the sum of their parts. Oneness isn't at the cost of their identity, but actually a result of it. The more they are one, the more they can be themselves as individuals. The more they are lovingly themselves, the more they are one.

Body/Spirit. Marriage teaches us that neither we nor God are supposed to melt away into a spiritual cloud, because marriage is emphatically body and spirit combined. You can't split people up that way, saying that either marriage is just physical (sex) or just spiritual (love). The two go together: you love each other through sex, and you have sex in love. So God, too, isn't a spiritual cloud: we see Him best in His Son, who had a body. Nor are we to withdraw from the physical world, into the spiritual: other religions emphasize that but Christianity does not. As Paul told us so emphatically, "Honor God with your bodies."

Sacrificial. A truly good marriage always involves sacrificing yourself for the good of the other. This, we find out, is the way God relates to us. too. Consider it: if you think of the gods of Egypt or Babylon, the stern masks of other-worldly creatures, what do you see? You see demands. Of course, that catches part of the character of God, but not all. Those Gods

A Love Story

never sacrificed for anyone: we sacrifice to them. But in Christianity the sacrifice is God's: He gave, and gives, His son. He sacrifices Himself so that our relationship to Him may grow.

Institutional. It is popular to think of God hating institutions. How could He work through a committee? Why would He use charts and budgets? The characteristic way God works is through lightning, through visions, through miracles.

But marriage flatly contradicts that. Of course, the institution is worth nothing in itself, but God uses it to make the model of His love for us, to create a new generation of creatures to love Him, and to give us our greatest chance for real intimacy with another human being. He does great things with this institution, cold and legal as it can be. So we learn that the way to see God work is not to go against all formulas, all institutions, but to ask God's Spirit to fill them — just as the love of a couple fills the marriage vows and makes them beautiful.

Celebratory. Marriage is enriched by a series of celebrations. A celebration is something that recalls, on a rhythmic basis, something that happened once. But celebrations aren't just memory: they take on a life of their own, and add to the original event.

Anniversaries are the obvious celebration of marriage. But Dwight `Small has suggested that intercourse itself be looked on as a celebration, and I like that idea. Each time husband and wife make love together they remember the beginning of it all: their promises to each other, and the way they've grown to understand and fulfill those promises (no one can understand even a fraction of his wedding vows when he makes them). They express that through sex. And sex itself becomes a fulfillment and participation in that once-for-all wedding ceremony.

God's relationship to us demands celebration, too: it's that good. We call it "The Lord's Supper," or "Communion," or "the Eucharist." It's a reminder of the once-for-all bond between us: we celebrate that bond which we've grown to understand more completely than we ever understood at first. And God celebrates with us: in fact, the bread and wine mingle us together. It is not an erotic experience, but it is certainly a celebration in which we "make love" and become "as one." Our relationship with Him demands celebration.

Love bound by promises. Marriage is passionate. Mad kisses, lying awake at night thinking of your loved one, hearts beating "each to each" are part of marriage. They are the beginning of marriage, certainly — and hopefully they continue.

But if they are to continue, they have to be bound by promises. We make vows that we expect to keep, and the law and the church enforce those promises. We speak our promises, too, so that the person we love can hear them. We write them down, so they can't change or be subject to argument about what really was said. These written promises form our wedding ceremony.

God, too, is passionate. He loves us with this kind of love: a fiery love, an emotion-filled love. But unlike pagan gods, who change from hot to cold like the weather, our God binds His will. He has promised us He will never leave us alone, never forsake us no matter how many mistakes we make, no matter how many faults we have. He loves us, and He has written down His marriage promises. They are written in the Bible, where they cannot change. And He swears that He will keep those promises. He swears by Himself.

* * * *

Can you see where this has taken us? We started by asking a few practical questions about sex. I tried to answer as simply and pragmatically as I could, but I couldn't leave things there. To truly appreciate sex, we have to go further. God made it, so we expect to find His fingerprints on it. We find more than that. His mark is not there by accident. Sex is a marriage portrait He has given us — a portrait of the marriage between Him and us. That is all the more reason why we should never abuse it.